The Fiction of South Asians in
North America and the Caribbean

The Fiction of South Asians in North America and the Caribbean

A Critical Study of English-Language Works Since 1950

Mitali P. Wong
and Zia Hasan

McFarland & Company, Inc., Publishers
Jefferson, North Carolina, and London

LIBRARY OF CONGRESS CATALOGUING-IN-PUBLICATION DATA

Wong, Mitali P., 1954–
  The fiction of South Asians in North America and the
Caribbean : a critical study of English-language works since
1950 / Mitali P. Wong and Zia Hasan.
    p.   cm.
  Includes bibliographical references and index.

  ISBN 0-7864-1925-3 (softcover : 50# alkaline paper) ∞

  1. American fiction—South Asian American authors—
History and criticism. 2. Caribbean fiction (English)—
South Asian authors—History and criticism. 3. South
Asians—Caribbean Area—Intellectual life. 4. South Asian
Americans—Intellectual life. 5. South Asians in literature.
6. Immigrants in literature. 7. Minorities in literature.
I. Hasan, Zia, 1953– II. Title.
PS153.S68W66   2004
813.009'8914—dc22   2004016411

British Library cataloguing data are available

©2004 Mitali P. Wong and Zia Hasan. All rights reserved

*No part of this book may be reproduced or transmitted in any form
or by any means, electronic or mechanical, including photocopying
or recording, or by any information storage and retrieval system,
without permission in writing from the publisher.*

On the cover: ©2004 PhotoSpin

Manufactured in the United States of America

McFarland & Company, Inc., Publishers
  Box 611, Jefferson, North Carolina 28640
    www.mcfarlandpub.com

To the next generation of
diasporic South Asian artists and
thinkers in the global village

Acknowledgments

The authors wish to thank Claflin University's Center for Excellence in Teaching, which provided summer research funding in 1999 and 2000 towards the exploration of this project. Special thanks are in order to Dr. Mohammed Yousef, Reference Librarian at Claflin University, for his help in obtaining materials. Thanks are also in order to Dr. Eugene F. Wong, Associate Professor of Sociology, South Carolina State University, for his scholarly discussions of the history of Asian American migration as well as some of the major social issues in twentieth-century Asian American literature and film.

For typing, editing, and research assistance, the authors wish to acknowledge Mr. Askia Hale, Ms. Paramita Pati, and Ms. Corinthia Rice. The epigraph from T.S. Eliot's poetry is inspired by the comments of the Bengali poet Bishnu Dey, whose essay "Mr. Eliot among the Arjunas" (anthologized in 1948 by Tambimuttu) contains the valid observation that Eliot's method and vision had a significant impact upon English language literary production in South Asia in the middle of the twentieth century. According to Bishnu Dey, Eliot "has been of great help in realizing this active, creative, dialectic of our tradition" (Tambimuttu, *T.S. Eliot: A Symposium* 99).

Contents

Acknowledgments	vii
Preface	1
1. Riddles of Time and Change: Marginality and Immigrant Fiction	5
2. Identity and the Indo-Caribbean Experience: Themes, Genres, and Characters in the Fiction of V.S. Naipaul and Samuel Selvon	16
3. Self-Definition and Difference: Ved Mehta and Ruth Prawer Jhabvala	29
4. The Immigrants' Search for Identity: Bharati Mukherjee and Chitra Banerjee Divakaruni	49
5. New Voices: Bapsi Sidhwa, Jhumpa Lahiri, and Other Emerging Fiction Writers	73
6. Another World, Another Time: The Fiction of Anita Desai, Amitav Ghosh, and Other Contemporary Novelists	89
7. Narratives of Exile: South Asian Writers in Canada	103
8. The Revival of Adolescent Fiction: From Dhan Gopal Mukerji to Mitali Perkins and Indi Rana	118
Works Cited	129
Bibliography	137
Index	143

Whatever we think and feel will colour what we say or do. He who fears, even unconsciously, or has his least little dream tainted with hate, will inevitably, sooner or later, translate these two qualities into his action. Therefore, my brothers, live courage, breathe courage and give courage. Think and feel love so that you will be able to pour out of yourselves peace and serenity so naturally as a flower gives forth fragrance.
  "Peace be unto all."

—Dhan Gopal Mukerji:
Gay-Neck: The Story of a Pigeon

Preface

Confused and confusing literary taxonomies surround the English-language fiction of writers who can trace their cultural ties to the region known as South Asia, which includes India, Pakistan, Bangladesh, Nepal, Sikkim, Bhutan, Sri Lanka, and perhaps peripherally, Afghanistan and Myanmar (Burma). An example of the difficulties of appropriate naming of English-language writers from South Asia in a global frame of reference came up at our school, Claflin University, when a faculty committee was finalizing the program for a reading on campus by the United Kingdom–based novelist Romesh Gunesekera. How should this document describe this guest speaker for the audience? Was he a Sri Lankan novelist, a British-Asian novelist, or a diasporic South Asian novelist? We decided to omit the label. This novelist's list of awards was impressive enough on the program information, especially the short-listing for the Booker Prize.

An example of similar confusion comes from the experience of one of the authors of this volume, who was reading Bharati Mukherjee's *Desirable Daughters* at a break between sessions of a regional workshop for English educators organized by the state's department of education. Attracted by the bright Indian design on the novel's cover, a friendly English teacher queried, "Is it East Indian?" The term itself was evocative of colonial times and of the voyages of early explorers. The questioner was provided the simple factual explanation that this was a new American novel and that the author was a well-known professor at Berkeley. At the International Short Story Conference in 2000 held at the University of Iowa, African American poet Amiri Baraka surprised a percentage of his audience by pointing out that more people (in terms of sheer numbers) possibly used the English language in India than in the United States. This demographic fact dispels the aura of the exotic and faraway conjured up by "East Indian," instead suggesting a large market for writers and publishers of English-language works that have South Asian connections.

It is evident that in our times we have a problem with the superficial packaging and labeling of writers and their texts. In the global culture of the twenty-first century, we are not always able to see beyond groups and group identities as we examine issues in literature. While the temporal and spatial dimensions of all art remain significant, we have probably reached a Babel-like situation in generating labels and taxonomies for authors and texts originating from the South Asian diaspora. Hence, the term "South Asian" in this study is an attempt to include numerous labels and would embrace both Bharati Mukherjee and Romesh Gunesekera, if contemporary British writers were included in the discussion along with American, Canadian, and Caribbean writers.

The title of this volume, *The Fiction of South Asians in North America and the Caribbean: A Critical Study of English-Language Works Since 1950*, has two clear defining components: one, the categories of writers included, and two, the regions from which the fiction is published. The geographical range includes the United States, Canada, and the Caribbean (mainly Trinidad). The writer categories include diasporic South Asian writers published in the United States, writers of South Asian ancestry born and raised in the Americas, and immigrant South Asian writers. The principles of selection and organization are not encyclopedic or survey-like; instead, writers have been chosen for the purpose of comparing common themes, narrative methods, genres, and sub-genres. Informative Web sites already exist that provide basic information for encyclopedic purposes, and print encyclopedias are also on their way.

The recognition of the need for a study such as this one came about six or seven years ago when we found library research itself to be a challenge because of the bewildering patterns of classification and shelving of South Asian literature at large university libraries. For instance, a South Asian Canadian writer of Caribbean origins could have some volumes of his work and related reference materials in the section on Caribbean literature and some among Canadian literature, irrespective of the fact that they were all published in Canada. A South Asian American writer who has written and published solely in the United States might be shelved among contemporary Indian writers. And the writings of Dhan Gopal Mukerji, one of the earliest Asian American novelists, have usually been placed among Indian literature on library shelves. Yet other challenges emerged as we researched the project, such as the limited first editions that are out of print and hard to locate, not to mention editions that were not for sale in the United States.

As we continued to work, we observed that while research and publication on individual South Asian authors seemed to be proliferating, very little existed in the way of comparative analysis of fictional methods.

We became convinced that there was a need to define the genre of South Asian fiction—its origins, its scope, and its global audience. With the 2000 Pulitzer Prize being awarded to South Asian American author Jhumpa Lahiri, and the 2001 Nobel Prize for Literature to V.S. Naipaul, who has been widely read and studied in the New World for over three decades, it has become clear that this growing body of fiction needs to be studied as a genre in all its complexity.

The study of South Asian fiction in America is inseparable from the study of Asian American fiction. Yet, surprisingly, current anthologies of Asian American literature intended for university courses exclude Dhan Gopal Mukerji (1890–1936), who received the Newbery Medal in 1928 for his novel *Gay-Neck: The Story of a Pigeon* (1927). Mukerji's autobiography, *Caste and Outcast* (republished in 2002), carries the fundamental message of tolerance and understanding between diverse groups, a message that remained outside of mainstream American life till the civil rights era. Common threads that run through Asian American literature can also be identified in South Asian writing: immigrant experiences, nostalgic memories of Asian countries, gender issues, intergenerational conflicts, struggles both inside and outside of the ethnic community, problems of place and displacement, and traditionalist ideologies versus assimilationist ideologies. The most striking difference in theme between South Asian literature in the Americas and Asian American literature is that South Asian writers do not address linguistic discrimination in any significant way, perhaps because most South Asian immigrants bring knowledge of English as the current language of global business—and as part of their common colonial legacy.

The focus of this study is on the last half century. The study is organized according to the pattern of South Asian migration to the New World, beginning with Indo-Caribbean authors such as the late Samuel Selvon and the celebrated V.S. Naipaul. The study continues with Ved Mehta and Ruth Prawer Jhabvala, long-term contributors to *The New Yorker*; the social criticism of Bharati Mukherjee and Chitra Divakaruni; and immigrant South Asian writers in the United States such as Amitav Ghosh, Anita Desai, Vikram Chandra, and Samrat Upadhyay. The next generation is represented by Jhumpa Lahiri, Akhil Sharma, and Mitali Perkins. Manil Suri, an Indian-born professor of mathematics in the United States who has written a best-selling novel, is included to demonstrate that this genre includes diverse talents. Residents of India such as Vikram Seth, Manju Kapur, and Indi Rana have been included as examples of writers published on three continents. An exclusion is represented by United Nations official Shashi Tharoor, whose political tales of the Indian subcontinent target mainly South Asian audiences. Major South Asian Canadian writers have been grouped as Indo-Canadian—Anita Rau Badami and Rohinton Mistry—and Indo-Caribbean—the late Harold Sonny Ladoo, Neil Bissoondath, and Rabindranath Maharaj.

In the absence of a canon of South Asian fiction in English, an attempt has been made to cover authors who have already received some form of public recognition such as awards, nominations for awards, or glowing reviews. However, we acknowledge that there may be unknown artists still waiting for recognition, and even as these lines are composed, new South Asian writers are writing and publishing their fiction. Writers and works have also been studied from a comparative point of view to define the characteristics of the genre.

This study therefore encapsulates vital information and essential critical discussion of a rich and diverse body of South Asian fiction written and or published in the Americas for a target audience of interested readers, beginning scholars, and educators of literature. The body of fiction studied is written in English and derived from the traditions of both British and American literature. In this aspect, the fiction is clearly different from fiction published in the many national and regional languages of South Asia that is composed for readers in South Asia who use a particular language. These regional works draw upon well-established literary traditions in those respective languages. For example, comparisons with fiction written in languages such as Hindi, Bengali, and Urdu, the national languages of India, Bangladesh, and Pakistan, illustrate the Western descent lines of South Asian English-language fiction written for a global readership. While ethnic characters and seemingly quaint cultural events provide interest to the reader, the primary themes and narrative methods remain universal.

1

Riddles of Time and Change: Marginality and Immigrant Fiction

> *These fragments I have shored against my ruins*
> *Why then Ile fit you. Hieronymo's mad againe.*
> *Datta. Dayadhvam. Damyata.*
> *Shantih shantih shantih*
> —T.S. Eliot: *The Waste Land*

Texts and Contexts

For more than half a century starting about 1950, American publishers and literary magazines such as *The New Yorker* have continued steadily to publish fiction with characters, settings, and themes related to southern Asia. The blending of different prose genres by South Asian writers such as V.S. Naipaul has been recognized by the Nobel Academy (cnn.com 1). The nonfictional narratives of Ved Mehta, a staff writer for *The New Yorker*, generated much interest at the time of their publication, as did the satiric Indo-Caribbean fiction of V.S. Naipaul. Recently, however, with the awarding of the 2001 Nobel Prize for Literature to Naipaul, and the growing recognition for the short fiction of 2000 Pulitzer prizewinner Jhumpa Lahiri, whose characters, plots, and themes deal with universal human experiences, South Asian fiction has achieved justifiable recognition as a sub-genre of American fiction. There is also an upcoming second generation of such fiction, in the genre of young adult fiction, manifest in such novels as Mitali Perkins's *The Sunita Experiment* (1993) and *The Roller Birds of Rampur* (1993). And contemporary short fiction writers such as Akhil Sharma and Samrat Upadhyay have made their way into anthologies of *Best American Short Stories* in 1998, 1999, and 2000.

While articles, conference papers, and collections of critical essays on individual authors proliferate, there is a clear need for a study of the sub-genre, or, better, the genre itself, its origins, its scope, as well as for the comparative analysis of the fictional methods of writers of South Asian fiction. Unlike publishers who have found a sufficient market for South Asian fiction, scholars (particularly South Asian scholars) have sometimes had difficulties in identifying either the nature of the audience for such fiction or its overall purpose. With the spread of the South Asian diaspora in the Caribbean, England, and North America, the publication of fiction written in the English language concerning South Asian characters in diverse cultural contexts has generally increased. Consequently, the classification of such fiction, its purpose, and even its language has presented problems for scholars.

South Asian scholars have formerly lumped all English-language fiction by and about South Asians in the postcolonial era under the somewhat misleading label of "Indo-Anglian literature." While "Indo-Anglian" is an attempt to distinguish South Asian postcolonial literature from the "Anglo-Indian" or colonial literature of Rudyard Kipling and E.M. Forster, for example, Rashna Singh's comprehensive and thorough study *The Imperishable Empire* (1988) uses the label of "Indo-Anglian" for writers as different from one another in themes, plots, and characterization as V.S. Naipaul, Ved Mehta, and Bharati Mukherjee.

Singh questions the sincerity and purpose of such writers as artists. She points out that writers such as Bharati Mukherjee and V.S. Naipaul do not identify with questions of self-image and self-identity that a formerly colonized people must confront (Singh 234). In this respect, Singh finds South Asian writers to be somewhat lacking when compared with African novelists such as Achebe and Ngugi, or even major Afro-Caribbean writers (234). She suggests that most Indo-Anglian writers de-familiarize the familiar aspects of South Asian settings by using the metaphors of "their colonial mentors" (234). While Singh is quite correct in suggesting the Ango-Indian influences on South Asian literature, she ignores the fact that both Mukherjee and Naipaul are social satirists who bear the influence of Charles Dickens. As a confirmed classic author in the genre of the novel in English, Dickens can hardly be described as "a colonial mentor."

More recently, Chelva Kanaganayakam has emphasized the marginality of diasporic South Asian fiction in English by stating that

> migration, exile, and marginality are often associated with the impulse to experiment. The consciousness that informs such writing arises from the cusp between what is acquired and inherited and so can hardly be called entirely Indian or totally Western. The

authors belong and do not belong, although some tend to accept this predicament more readily than others [*Counterrealism* 22].

Thus the dilemmas regarding taxonomy and canon continue for scholars of South Asian fiction.

The problems in critical analysis arise from limitations within the concepts of political correctness adopted by postcolonialists who castigate authors who seem to defy the structures and political agendas of postcolonialist criticism. Naipaul has not been in favor with Third World postcolonialists (Lichtenstein 1). Singh contends that Ved Mehta is not interesting to South Asian audiences, in the process demeaning Ved Mehta's long career with *The New Yorker* and his established American reading public:

> Ved Mehta's endless autobiographies and accounts of his relatives ... are of interest to historians, social scientists, and anthropologists. But while there is ample provision of authenticity, there is little artistry. It is doubtful, in fact, if the author would have enjoyed his literary success, or even found a publisher, had he been an American, or raised in America. For the foreign reader, his narratives of an Indian childhood are narratives of faraway lands. For the Indian reader, they are simply boring [*Imperishable Empire* 14].

Similarly, Kenneth Ramchand has clearly pointed out that the picture of East Indian family life painted in Naipaul's *A House for Mr. Biswas* no longer exists in Trinidad even though the socio-historical past the novel's setting draws upon may be relevant (*The West Indian Novel* 189). Both critics are missing the bigger picture because their perspectives are limited by the tunnel vision of established western literary canon.

Ved Mehta's narratives of his Indian childhood and Naipaul's comic medley of characters and strange scenarios in his Indo-Caribbean fiction develop characters and themes of universal human interest. Undoubtedly, their mastery of English prose style is a legacy of their ties to a colonial past. Niaz Zaman states very aptly that "Caliban's children, the generation of midnight's children, like Rushdie and Tharoor, refuse to be awed by the language in which they write—even when it is, as Tharoor's narrator suggests, the only language in which a writer can write, and even when it is distorted" (*A Divided Legacy* 236). This mastery of style has actually proved an asset for South Asian writers in getting published in America, where English has not been the first language of most Asian immigrant groups.

In a recent study of Samuel Selvon's novels, Roydon Salick points out that postcolonial theory tends to generalize political issues, ignoring differences of race, class, and gender among formerly colonized peoples (2). Salick also observes very aptly:

> There is, too, an alarming tendency now to prioritize the statement of theory over the close reading of the text and to allow theory to run roughshod over works, sometimes willfully distorting, sometimes blatantly misreading the text [*The Novels of Samuel Selvon* 2].

The methodology used in this study seeks to balance both texts and contexts by remaining close to textual evidence to avoid distorted readings of historically and culturally complex issues.

South Asian Immigration to North America and the Caribbean

South Asian writing in America covers several genres among which fiction is the earliest, with Dhan Gopal Mukerji as its earliest acclaimed exponent. Dhan Gopal Mukerji (1890–1936) won the Newbery Medal in 1928 for his novel *Gay-Neck: The Story of A Pigeon* (1927). Mukerji's successful American literary career included the publication of more than twenty books of nonfiction, fiction, poetry, drama, translations, and children's stories (Wallia 1). He was inspired by the writings of Mahatma Gandhi and Rabindranath Tagore (the first South Asian writer to win the Nobel Prize for Literature) and had strong emotional links to India's freedom movement in the 1920s and 1930s. He was deeply conscious of the differences between East and West, and the New- and Old-World cultures. His career ended with his suicide at the age of forty-six (Chhaya 1). Mukerji's daring autobiography, *Caste and Outcast* (republished in 2002), includes his traditional Hindu Brahmin upbringing, his arrival in America and his experiences as a student and a worker in America, his marriage to fellow Stanford student Pat Dugan, the birth of their son, and Mukerji's early career. Dhan Gopal Mukerji's overall message is of tolerance and understanding between diverse groups, a message that is also emphasized in *Gay-Neck: The Story of a Pigeon*.

Another early writer of South Asian origin to achieve recognition in America was the poet Thurairajah Tambimuttu, a close associate of T.S. Eliot. A Tamil from Sri Lanka, Tambimuttu became an influential artist in England in the 1940s by founding and editing the magazine *Poetry London*. Arriving on the New York literary scene in the mid–1950s, Tambimuttu started to publish *Poetry London–New York*. Although he achieved recognition swiftly among American poets in the 1950s and 1960s, the magazine lost its financial support and Tambimuttu returned to England, where he died in 1983 (Sonnenberg 1–2).

While South Asian poetry continues to receive attention — recent poets in this group include names such as Meena Alexander and the versatile Chitra Banerjee Divakaruni, who is also noted for her fiction — the literary genres that have proved most popular among South Asian writers are the novel and the short story. Essayists are not absent either; the best-known contemporary essayist is probably Pico Iyer.

The history of South Asian fiction in America is closely tied to the history of the South Asian diaspora in the New World. Significant numbers of South Asians migrated to America later than other Asian American groups — Chinese, Japanese, Filipino, Korean, Hawaiian-Asian, Vietnamese, Malaysian and others. Other than the contributions of Dhan Gopal Mukerji, the beginnings of Asian American fiction in America can be found in early twentieth-century novels such as Etsu Sugimoto's *A Daughter of the Narikin* (1932) and *A Daughter of the Nohfu* (1935). The beginnings of the continuous publication of significant South Asian fiction in the New World have to be traced to the Caribbean, where "Starting in the 1830s poor Indians were recruited as indentured laborers to the sugar plantations of the West Indies to replace African slave labor" (Lessinger 9). In contrast, South Asians were not welcome in the U.S. or Canada in the late nineteenth and early twentieth century. Lessinger points out that "from 1850 to 1960, only some 13,500 Indians had entered the U.S. legally" (3). Shirley Geok-lin Lim also notes:

> The first recorded major influx of Asians to the United States occurred in 1848, after the news of the discovery of gold in California reached China. Anti-Asian sentiment began as early as 1850, with the onset of legislation to tax, contain, discriminate against, and exclude first the Chinese, then all Asians from U.S. soil [*Asian-American Literature* 1].

South Asian migration to America, then, is largely a phenomenon of the last three decades, coming as a sequel to the revision of anti–Asian immigration laws in 1968. Sociologist Johanna Lessinger categorizes the South Asian immigrants as a diverse group:

> Today some of these Indo-Caribbeans or Indo-Africans have migrated again in the last 30 years to Britain, Canada, and the U.S., partly as a result of ethnic conflict in their newly independent countries. Today the presence of people Bhachu calls "twice-migrants" (1985) in the U.S., linked to, but not wholly part of the Indian-born migrant population, suggests the long history and

the complexity of Indian migration. It also suggests the inadequacy of census categories based on race/ethnicity, since some of those who appear under the "Asian Indian" category in the U.S. are actually descendants of Indians who went to the Caribbean or Africa, and then re-migrated to the U.S. [*From the Ganges to the Hudson* 9].

Hence, a study of the emergence of South Asian fiction in the New World appropriately begins with Indo-Caribbean fiction.

South Asian writing shares many of the same concerns and characteristics of Asian American literature as a whole. Shirley Geok-lin Lim identifies the following principal thematic concerns in Asian American literature: the immigration experience, Asian affiliations, struggles and recognition, the individual inside/against the ethnic community, gender identities, gender relationships, parents and families, American place and displacement, and language and vision (xvi). Lim also points out that Asian American narratives share common themes of coming-to-America experiences with Italian or Central and Eastern European immigrants' writing (1–2). There are essential differences between the immigrant experiences of Asian groups and European groups in America as reflected in literature, however, that are traceable to the non-western origins of Asians (Lim 2).

For the purposes of this study, fiction writers have been grouped by time, place, and thematic similarities, with due consideration given to Caribbean origins, Asian American immigrant narratives, and nostalgic tales about South Asia by expatriate authors. The texts selected for analysis range from Caribbean to American and Canadian, with an emphasis upon the last fifty years.

Language and Difference

The fact that the emergence of South Asian fiction in America occurs simultaneously with South Asian migration during the last thirty years is a clear reminder of the presence of an educated reading public in the diasporic South Asian community itself, as well as the larger American reading public. A recent article in *Time* provides supporting facts: first, "Indian immigrants say they fit into corporate America because they already speak English," and secondly, "According to the Center for Immigration Studies, only 3 percent of Indian arrivals lack a high school education, and 75 percent of working Indians are college graduates" ("The Golden Diaspora," *Time*, June 19, 2000, B28). Lessinger's earlier study expands on this:

1. Riddles of Time and Change

The most striking advantage Indian immigrants bring with them is fluency in English. After 200 years under British colonial domination, India's urban middle class values higher education as a route to social mobility.... This gives urban middle-class Indians privileged access to the international worlds of science, technology, finance and management, whose common language across national borders is now English. It also means that almost 45% of Indian immigrants here use English even at home [15].

Ironically, the mastery of English prose, historically a badge of subordination in the Old World, is transformed into a symbol of freedom in the New World, a freedom to explore the interplay of *differance* and to resolve a variety of differences and conflicts in the New World. Although the English-speaking culture of South Asia is a legacy of the colonial past (as postcolonialists continue to remind scholars), in the context of Asian American writing, the English-language heritage of South Asian fiction writers frees them to a certain extent from concerns of linguistic discrimination and the continuing seesaw of bilingual and bicultural differences that have been prevalent thematic concerns of Asian American literature for almost half a century. As Homi K. Bhabha reminds readers in *The Location of Culture*:

> The representation of difference must not be read as the reflection of *pre-given* ethnic or cultural traits set in the fixed tablet of tradition. The social articulation of difference, from the minority perspective, is a complex, on-going negotiation that seeks to authorize cultural hybridities that emerge in moments of historical transformation [2].

In this study "difference" is used in the sense of Jacques Derrida's term *differance*. Derrida's *differance* is one of a group of terms by which the philosopher expresses his "admiration for the proliferating, the elusive, the allusive, the ever-self-recontextualizing" (Cambridge *History of Literary Criticism*, Vol. 8, 1995). In *Of Grammatology*, Derrida maintains that

> reading and writing, the production or interpretation of signs, the text in general as fabric of signs, allow themselves to be confined within secondariness. They are preceded by a truth, or a meaning already constituted by and within the element of the logos [16].

This study of South Asian fiction explores texts and contexts and the rich interplay of *differance* that forever creates new meanings in the New

World. Post-structuralist analysis also requires the exploration of who writes, for whom, and why, as well as the study of the plurality of narratives. Roland Barthes returns readers to the "raw material" of literature—language: "Who speaks? Who writes? We still lack a sociology of language" (*Critical Essays* 142).

The study of the emergent canon of South Asian fiction places the analyst in a predicament well defined by Roland Barthes:

> Faced with the infinity of narratives, the multiplicity of standpoints—historical, psychological, sociological, aesthetic, etc.—from which they can be studied, the analyst finds himself in more or less the same situation as Saussure confronted by the heterogeneity of language [*langage*] and seeking to extract a principle of classification and a central focus for description from the apparent confusion of the individual messages. Keeping simply to modern times, the Russian Formalists, and Levi-Strauss have taught us to recognize the following dilemma: either a narrative is merely a rambling collection of events, in which case nothing can be said about it other than referring back to the storyteller's (the author's) art ... or else it shares with other narratives a common structure which is open to analysis, no matter how much patience its formulation requires [*Image, Music, Text* 80].

The analyst must therefore consider the author, the language, the plurality of narratives within fictional texts, and "their historical, geographical, and cultural diversity" (*Image, Music, Text* 81). More recently Homi Bhabha states that

> The linguistic difference that informs any cultural performance is dramatized in the common semiotic account of the disjuncture between the subject of a proposition (*enonce*) and the subject of enunciation, which is not represented in the statement but which is the acknowledgement of its discursive embeddedness and address, its cultural positionality, its reference to a present time and a specific space [*The Location of Culture* 36].

Thus, this work on South Asian fiction in America is exploratory because the body of writing examined is only about fifty years old. Also, the body of fiction is frequently cross-referenced with literature in English from the Indian subcontinent as well as diasporic South Asian literature from the United Kingdom and other parts of the British Commonwealth. The study is selective in its choice of authors and their specific works rather than a historical survey of the genre. The analysis demonstrates that clear paradigms of narratology, culture, and society are identifiable in South Asian fiction published in America in the last fifty years. This study examines recurring themes, motifs, and narrative methodologies in the newly emerging but distinct body of South Asian fiction in America published for American audiences. Thus, Shashi Tharoor's Commonwealth Writers' award-winning *The Great Indian Novel* (1992) is excluded because its themes and characters focus upon satirizing Indian politics and history for international readers as well as readers in the Indian subcontinent. According to Tharoor: "In some ways, the writing has helped me to reclaim and reinvent a sense of my Indianness which I believe has spoken to Indians in ways that I find very gratifying" (Kreisler 1).

Writers, Margins and Paradigms

The work begins with Indo-Caribbean novelists Samuel Selvon and V. S. Naipaul, and continues with Ved Mehta and Ruth Prawer Jhabvala, steady contributors to *The New Yorker* for over three decades. In the eighties and nineties, satire and social criticism are predominant in the fiction of Bharati Mukherjee and Chitra Divakaruni. New voices of difference surface in the short fiction of Akhil Sharma and Samrat Upadhyay. Bapsi Sidhwa successfully evokes a multi-layered perception of *otherness* or marginality. Around 2000, in the short fiction of Jhumpa Lahiri, character development and exploration of psychological dilemmas attain human universality that transcends historical, geographical, and cultural differences. Expatriate and diasporic authors of South Asian origin who create tales that range in tone from the satiric to the nostalgic include Anita Desai, Amitav Ghosh, Vikram Chandra, the late Harold Sonny Ladoo, Rabindranath Maharaj, Neil Bissoondath, Anita Rau Badami and Rohinton Mistry. It is interesting to note that some of the writers—Vikram Seth, Manju Kapur, and Indi Rana, for example—are residents of India who are published on three continents, indicating the global audience for South Asian fiction in English.

A secondary developing sub-genre emerges in the young adult fiction of Mitali Perkins and Indi Rana, who revive Dhan Gopal Mukerji's interest in the concerns of youth by depicting the adolescent conflicts of second-generation South Asians in the New World and the West. Parallels and contrasts with the canon of British and American fiction are discussed in the following chapters along with the effect on human lives of social changes such as the women's movement both in America and in South Asian societies.

There are clearly discernible parallels in this body of literature with earlier American immigrant writers such as Isaac Bashevis Singer, who stated in his 1978 Nobel lecture: "While the poet entertains he continues to search for eternal truths, for the essence of being. In his own fashion he tries to solve the riddle of time and change, to find an answer to suffering, to reveal love in the very abyss of cruelty and injustice" (2). The experiences of marginality perceived by fictional protagonists, the awareness of belonging to two different cultures but not wholly to either one, is reiterated in the Jewish American fiction of Saul Bellow. Bellow's early novels—*Dangling Man* (1944), *The Victim* (1947), *The Adventures of Augie March* (1953), and *Herzog* (1964)—focus upon protagonists who experience self-division and a heightened awareness of their own marginality. The immigrant acquires a heightened sense of what Paulo Freire terms "cultural invasion" (cultural domination) of one group in society by another (*The Pedagogy of the Oppressed* 133). Freire writes, "For cultural invasion to succeed, it is essential that those invaded become convinced of their intrinsic inferiority.... If those who are invaded consider themselves inferior, they must necessarily recognize the superiority of the invaders" (134). The traditionalist immigrants resist assimilation or cultural synthesis while the assimilationist immigrants seek out ways of belonging to the culture of the country of their adoption. The idealized model of resolving differences is, of course, "cultural synthesis" (Freire 164).

    The contrast between the confined gender roles of older societies and the comparative freedom of women in America has been addressed by Asian American writer Maxine Hong Kingston in *The Woman Warrior* (1976) and by Amy Tan in *The Joy Luck Club* (1989) and *The Kitchen God's Wife* (1991). Issues of gender and race are woven into the characters' perceptions of marginality in several works of South Asian fiction. With regard to the subordination of women, the South Asian male is demonized in the novels of Bharati Mukherjee and Chitra Divakaruni in a manner reminiscent of Tan and Kingston. Ruth Jhabvala and Sam Selvon depict South Asian males as objects of desire for European women but social subordinates at the same time. Occasional episodes of anti–Asian racism are depicted in the fiction of Divakaruni and Mukherjee, emphasizing the fictional protagonists' perceptions of marginality. And in "One But of Many," Naipaul's Santosh refuses the title of "Soul Brother" given to him by the African Americans among whom he lives (61).

    Naipaul's 2001 Nobel lecture cites Proust on the necessity of separating "the writer as writer and the writer as a social being" as he rationalizes his interest in writing about "areas of darkness," another name for cultural conflict, *otherness*, and marginality (1–7). Emergent paradigms that surface in contemporary South Asian fiction reveal that the writing is non-documentary in that most of the works de-emphasize the ethnic in favor of universal human experiences. This body of fiction perhaps should not be classified as either "postcolonial" or "Indo-Anglian" in its literary heritage. The overall descent lines are clearly American. However, themes and concerns of a global nature also surface time and again in these writings. A recurring subject is the violence latent in postcolonial societies such as those in South Asia. To this subject of violence may be applied Frantz Fanon's view that violence is part of the conditions of postcolonial existence, that "decolonisation" is always a violent condition (*The Wretched of the Earth* 29).

The fictional protagonists of South Asian writers are frequently anti-heroes analogous to the *shlemiels* (losers) of Jewish American fiction, characters who fail to realize their versions of the American dream. The immigrant protagonists are both traditionalists and assimilationists, ceaselessly pondering their own *différance* and marginality, especially in the short stories of Jhumpa Lahiri, Akhil Sharma, and Samrat Upadhyay.

The focus in this study is upon the South Asian experience in the New World as well as in colonial and postcolonial settings as depicted in the fiction of the last half century. Overall, a body of American fiction with distinctive features, pregnant with multiple layers of meaning, has been born as a result of South Asian migration.

2

Identity and the Indo-Caribbean Experience: Themes, Genres, and Characters in the Fiction of V.S. Naipaul and Samuel Selvon

Indo-Caribbean writers comprise two groups: those who wrote while resident in their island homes, and those who recreated their Caribbean memories from New World countries of adoption. In the first group, V.S. Naipaul and Samuel Selvon began their novelistic careers exploring the Indo-Caribbean experience in their native Trinidad. Naipaul was to move to other subjects when he relocated to England. Samuel Selvon also moved to a wider canvas as an immigrant author in Canada although he returned to his native Trinidad toward the end of his life. The second group of Indo-Caribbean writers are expatriates permanently resident in Canada, such as the late Harold Sonny Ladoo, Neil Bissoondath, and Rabindranath Maharaj, whose fictional methods are discussed in chapter seven.

While Naipaul's narrative method is one of satire with the creation of a vast array of typecast characters, Selvon is sympathetic to the immigrant's struggle in his/her land of adoption. Naipaul's penetrating satires of Third World cultures have aroused much controversy because he is neither politically correct nor sympathetic. In his Nobel lecture, Naipaul alludes to his special interest in writing about little-known Third World environments he calls areas of "darkness." David Lichtenstein aptly comments that

> Critics laud Naipaul for the extraordinary vision that marks his writing. Perhaps due to his status as a rootless wanderer, as a man without a heritage to hold sway over him, Naipaul consistently knocks down idealized views of the places he journeys to, be they

2. Identity and the Indo-Caribbean Experience 17

England, Trinidad, or Africa, in favor of a more complex, bitter sometimes even contradictory truth.... Be it via the humor of his earlier books or the dark cynical psychology of later efforts, V.S. Naipaul has time and again used his honest and penetrating vision, coupled with an extraordinary command of the English language and its traditions, to paint portraits of the outcast roaming through the civilizations of the world [www.postcolonialweb.org/caribbean/naipaul/bio.html].

Knighted in 1989, Vidiadhar Surajprasad Naipaul was born in Trinidad on August 17, 1932. His family was of Indian Hindu Brahmin origin, and his father was a journalist. Naipaul began his education in Port of Spain. In 1950, he won a scholarship to Oxford University. He started his career as a writer on graduation from the university. Although Naipaul has lived largely in Britain since then, he has traveled worldwide and has written about his own experiences of exile and rootlessness. His themes and characters encapsulate the New World immigrant experience of South Asians. Naipaul's funny and rich novelistic creations of life in the expatriate South Asian community of the Trinidad he grew up in have enjoyed an established place with American readers since the nineteen fifties in a category somewhat loosely termed "Caribbean fiction" or "West Indian fiction." Lillian Feder comments that

> In Naipaul's work the development of selfhood, actual or fictive, is continuous exploration, inner narratives with referential affiliations among autobiography, journalism, and fiction.... His fiction and nonfiction are complementary explorations of processes of selfhood stimulated and impaired by the nexus of familial, political, social, and cultural forces to which they are subject [*Naipaul's Truth* 8].

Naipaul's resolution of differences between his early life in Trinidad and his adoption of London as his intellectual house is chronicled in *The Enigma of Arrival* (1987), where he summarizes the condition of South Asians in the Caribbean countries:

> We were immemorially people of the countryside, far from the courts of princes, living according to rituals we didn't always understand yet were unwilling to dishonor because that would cut us off from the past, the sacred earth, the gods. Those earth rites went back far. They would always have been partly mysterious ... would have been easier to accept too, because forty years before, it would have all been so much poorer, so much closer to the Indian past; houses, roads, vehicles, clothes. Now money had touched us

all—like a branch of a tree or a twig dipped in gold, according to some designer's extravagant whim, and made to keep the shape of the twig or the leaf. Generations of a new kind of education had separated us from the past; and travel; and history. And the money that had come to our island, from oil and natural gas [351].

The Nobel foundation considered *The Enigma of Arrival* to be Naipaul's masterpiece. In it Naipaul also concedes that he repeatedly turned to memories of his native Port of Spain for the materials of his fictional world, even though "Trinidad itself, the starting point, the center—could no longer hold me" (154). He reflects upon the influence of Dickens's fictional techniques, such as that of applying fantasy to his surroundings, on his own development as a writer:

> Years later, looking at Dickens during a time when I was writing hard myself, I felt I understood a little more about Dickens's unique power as a describer of London, and all his difference from all the other writers about London. I felt that when as a child, far away I read the early Dickens and was able to be with him to enter the dark city of London, it was partly because I was taking my own simplicity to his, fitting my own fantasies to his....
>
> To Dickens, this enriching of one's known surroundings by fantasy was one of the good things about fiction. And it was apt that Dickens's childlike vision should have given me, with my own child's ideas, my abstract education and my very simple idea of my vocation, an illusion of complete knowledge of the city where I expected this vocation to flower [*Enigma* 133–134].

And indeed, the influence of Dickens is very evident in Naipaul's early fiction: the Dickensian multitudes of comic characters, the use of typecast characters, the recreation of local speech and idiom, the episodic comic plot structures, the creation of an enduring fantasy world in Naipaul's Trinidad with a focus on the "little India" of the South Asian immigrant community.

Elsewhere in *The Enigma of Arrival*, Naipaul notes that from about 1950 onwards, the great cities of the world were to become culturally mixed with immigrants from all the continents (141). While Naipaul began his observations in London, the diasporic experiences of various non–European groups are a continuing interest in the postcolonial era.

However, not always does the cultural mixing bring the happiness that is supposed to be associated with freedom. In "One But of Many," the first story in the collection *In a Free State* (1971), Naipaul creates the first-person narrative of an Indian domestic named Santosh. Santosh arrives

2. Identity and the Indo-Caribbean Experience   19

in Washington, D.C., as the servant of an Indian diplomat. His job keeps him housebound day in and day out. He escapes and begins work in an Indian restaurant, thereby becoming an illegal alien. Living in a condition of chronic fear, Santosh decides to marry an African American woman who works as a maid. As he becomes a legal resident by marriage, he moves into the ghetto only to feel forever alienated in the New World of his adoption:

> Once there were rumours of new burnings, someone scrawled in white paint on the pavement outside my house; *Soul Brother.* I understand the words; but I feel, brother to what or whom? I was once part of the flow, never thinking of myself a presence. Then I looked in the mirror and decided to be free. All that my freedom has brought me is the knowledge that I have a face and have a body, that I must feed and clothe this body for a certain number of years. Then it will be over [61].

In his perception of alienation as central to the postmodern existence of the diasporic South Asian, Naipaul's Santosh has similarities to Selvon's Tiger. Also like Tiger, who experiences the beginnings of political awareness, Naipaul's *The Suffrage of Elvira* (1958) creates a comic Dickensian world peopled with a multitude of characters in a community gearing up for a local election:

> Things were crazily mixed up in Elvira. Everybody, Hindus, Muslims and Christians owned a Bible; the Hindus and Muslims looking on it, if anything, with greater awe. The Spaniards and some of the negroes celebrated the Hindu festival of lights. Someone had told them Lakshmi, the goddess of prosperity, was being honoured; they placed small earthen lamps in their money-boxes and waited, as they said, for the money to breed. Everybody celebrated the Muslim festival of Hosein. In fact, when Elvira was done with the religious festivals, there were few straight days left [74].

In this early novel there is little character development or conventional analysis. The narrative abounds in comic episodes with the careful intertwining of several narrative strands. The novel concludes with resolution of the action on the level of the plot, rather than in terms of character development:

> So Harbans won the election and the insurance company lost a Jaguar. Chittaranjan lost a son-in-law and Dhaniram lost a daughter-in-law. Elvira lost Lorkhoor and Lorkhoor won a reputation.

> Elvira lost Mr. Cuffy. And Preacher lost his deposit [*Suffrage of Elvira* 240].

Like *The Suffrage of Elvira*, Naipaul's *A House for Mr. Biswas* (1961) also presents a vast array of typecast characters set in the East Indian community of Trinidad. However, *A House for Mr. Biswas* develops the central character Mr. Biswas much more fully than any characters in Naipaul's earlier or later fiction. Often considered to be Naipaul's fictional masterpiece, *A House for Mr. Biswas* perhaps contains partially autobiographical materials. Helen Hayward has explored the raw materials of Naipaul's fiction and nonfiction to show that the novel is based on the life of the author's father Seepersad, and that the model for Hanuman House comes from the Capildeo family, the author's maternal family who lived in the Lion House (Hayward 8).

The novel uses the point of view of an omniscient first-person narrator who chronicles the protagonist's life from birth to death. Mr. Biswas's lifelong struggle is one of resolving differences within himself and between him and external forces. Born the son of a laborer, he turns out to be different from his siblings:

> But Mr. Biswas never went to work on the estates. Events which were to occur presently led him away from that. They did not lead him to riches, but made it possible for him to console himself later in life with the *Meditations* of Marcus Aurelius while he rested on the Slumberking bed in the one room which contained most of his possessions [*A House for Mr. Biswas* 23].

After his father's early death, he begins to perceive issues of his own identity and difference. His only claims to social prestige are linked to his profession of journalism, and his married status as a Tulsi son-in-law. He well realizes the ambiguities of his social position:

> In Tara's house he was respected as a Brahmin and pampered; yet as soon as the ceremony was over and he had taken the gifts of cloth and left, he became once more a labourer's child—father's occupation; labourer was the entry on the birth certificate F.Z. Ghany had sent—living with a penniless mother in one room of a mud hut. And throughout life his position was like that [*A House for Mr. Biswas* 45].

Because of his physical frailty, he is apprenticed to a priest for training in performing rituals. His tasks are described in great detail with a touch of comedy:

2. Identity and the Indo-Caribbean Experience   21

> He took around the brass plate with the lighted camphor; the devout dropped a coin on the plate, brushed the flame with their fingers to their forehead.... When the ceremonies were over and the feeding of the Brahmins began, he was seated next to pundit Jairam; and when Jairam had eaten and belched and asked for more, it was Mr. Biswas who mixed the bicarbonate of soda for him [*A House for Mr. Biswas* 47].

Mohun Biswas's apprenticeship with the priest Jairam is brief and ends abruptly when Biswas accidentally soils Jairam's oleander tree with his feces (46–47). Biswas then moves into the Tulsi household when he marries Shama, one of Mrs. Tulsi's daughters. The portrait of the Tulsi family is one of the strongest satires of the Hindu extended family household ever written inside or outside the Indian subcontinent. Excessive care is lavished upon the family's oldest son, described as "the elder god," who wears a crucifix because it is regarded as a valuable charm among other charms that he wears symbolizing his special position in the family (113). In this way Naipaul ridicules the superstitions prevalent among the Hindus of Trinidad. The novel has further observations on the inferior status of women in comparison to men in Trinidad's South Asian community:

> most of the women he knew were like Sushila, the widowed Tulsi daughter. She talked with pride of the beatings she had received from her short-lived husband, she regarded them as a necessary part of her training and often attributed the decay of Hindu society in Trinidad to the rise of the timorous, weak, non-wife beating class of husband [*A House for Mr. Biswas* 133].

Mr. Biswas, of course, is not empowered like the macho South Asian men of the past. Rather he has to put up with nagging, and he is in awe of women such as Mrs. Tulsi and Tara (133). While the Tulsi women are all caricatures, Mr. Biswas continues to sense his powerlessness over his own life as a Tulsi son-in-law managing a Tulsi shop (143).

The novel develops as a *bildungsroman* of a kind that could be transferred into almost any cultural setting, as the protagonist struggles to build an independent career as a journalist and to own a home of his own. Ironically, as soon as Biswas moves with his wife and children into a modest home, he is suddenly stricken with heart disease in his mid-forties [*A House for Mr. Biswas* 528–529].

Biswas takes long leaves of absence from the newspaper. *The Sentinel* puts him on half-pay (529). His daughter Savi returns home from university to become the family provider when Biswas loses his job. The change in the patriarchal structure of this South Asian family is evident.

There is also change in *The Sentinel*, where his obituary headline is the simple "JOURNALIST DIES SUDDENLY" instead of "ROVING REPORTER PASSES ON" as he had hoped. As an unknown citizen of the New World whose joys and sorrows are chronicled, Biswas is related not only to Dickens's heroes but to the antiheroes of mid-twentieth-century American literature such as Arthur Miller's Willy Loman, as well as to the common man featured in the works of other Caribbean novelists such as Braithwaite and Selvon.

The late Samuel Selvon's poetry and fiction is frequently quoted along with the works of Derek Walcott and V.S. Naipaul among significant works of West Indian literature. Although Selvon concerned himself with West Indian characters, much of his writing focused on the immigrant experience, ranging from the economic, social, and cultural problems faced by Black West Indians in England to those of the expatriate Indo-Caribbean farmers. Samuel Selvon himself left Trinidad to settle in Canada, thereby joining the diasporic writers of South Asian origin on the North American continent who examine the quest for identity in the South Asian immigrant's experience.

Victor Ramraj uses the sociological terms *traditionalist* and *assimilationist* to define the behaviors and philosophies of Indo-Caribbean immigrants: "The conflict between the assimilationists and the traditionalists often disrupts community and family life, with traumatic consequences for the individuals" ("Still Arriving" 78). Ramraj's definition of the experiences of Indo-Asian immigrants in literature may be applied to several contemporary portraits of the South Asian American predicament, including those of the other fiction writers discussed in the following chapters. Samuel Selvon (who later moved to Canada) is one of the earliest of these immigrant Asian authors.

Victor Ramraj's definition of the Indo-Caribbean experience encapsulates the larger conflicts experienced by immigrants from South Asia on the North American continent itself. According to Ramraj,

> A prominent aspect of the early and current Indo-Caribbean experience as depicted by Caribbean writers of East Indian extraction is the Indo-Caribbeans' sense of marginality in their adopted homes, be it the Caribbean itself or the European and North American countries to which they migrated. In the Caribbean, they are late arrivers, whose deeply rooted culture kept them apart from and prevented easy assimilation into the dominant British culture that was imposed on the colonies. Those who came to accept the assimilation as an inevitable course are depicted as perpetual travelers in a constant state of arriving [77–78].

2. Identity and the Indo-Caribbean Experience

To put Ramraj's definition in a larger context, the South Asian immigrants often find themselves in a traditionalist immigrant community whose "deeply rooted" non–Western culture keeps them marginalized. Those who seek to assimilate and to thereby escape the traditionalists' inevitable acceptance of marginalization become interesting subjects for fiction writers, who depict their dreams, conflicts, and failures.

At moments of stress and crisis, the traditionalists dream of returning to their communities of origin, a dream that is seldom translated into action because of a real fear of reverse culture shock. The dream, therefore, remains an archetypal desire to return to the mother (*regressus ad uterum*). The Asians' desire to return provides a clear contrast to Black African Americans' roots and lost culture in Africa. In the context of Caribbean fiction, Ramraj states,

> While the Indo-Caribbean assimilationists try to escape an entrenched culture that cocoons and imprisons them, the Afro-Caribbeans, whose ancestors virtually lost their culture under centuries of British cultural domination, seek their identity by going back to Africa and by rediscovering the folk, where their Africanness lies in vestigial form.... And while the Afro-Caribbeans are, to use Edward Kamau Brathwaite's term, *arrivants*, however dislocated and ambivalent, the Indo-Caribbean assimilationists are perpetual *arrivers*, who find themselves at the harbor contemplating the enigma of their arrival ["Still Arriving" 84].

Samuel Selvon explores the inner life of the Indo-Caribbean *arrivers* in Trinidad. Selvon's South Asians are mainly peasants growing sugarcane. From 1845 to 1917, some 143,939 indentured workers from the Gangetic plain of northern India arrived in Trinidad (Barratt 105). These immigrants were agricultural workers in plantations on whom the sugar industry depended. In the latter half of the nineteenth century, the East Indians were about one quarter of Trinidad's population. However, the East Indians continued to view themselves as "temporary" dwellers in their land of adoption. They fiercely protected their culture and saw themselves as fortune hunters amidst an alien culture. There are clear similarities in the behaviors of South Asian immigrants in the West Indies and in South Africa.

Samuel Selvon was born into the diasporic Trinidadian Indian community in 1923. His mother was part Indian, part Scottish. His father was an Indian dry goods merchant. Selvon lived in western Canada for many years in his later life. He died on April 16, 1995, in his native Trinidad. Obituaries classified Selvon as a folk poet rather than a novelist. Indeed, he had turned more towards drama and poetry in the later phases of his writing career. An article on the West Indian diaspora in *The Economist* (Dec. 10, 1994) lists Derek Walcott, V.S. Naipaul, and Samuel Selvon as the three greatest West Indian authors. The anonymous article provides a reminder that Selvon's earliest recognition was for his London fiction:

> The picture he draws in "The Lonely Londoners" of West Indians in the 1950's could hardly be bettered. Here are all the bleak circumstances of post-war London. Racism is rife; the weather is appalling; the chance of earning a decent living is negligible. But still his exiled West Indians survive: cunning, resourceful, roguish, playful, indomitable ["A Song of Lost Islands" 93].

Unlike the novels about Afro-Caribbean immigrants spread through his career, Selvon's chronicles of the South Asian peasant life in Trinidad belong to the earlier phase of his fiction. Selvon's young Trinidadian farmer Tiger is a precursor to the many Asian American fictional characters who search for a new identity in a new world. The novels that center upon Tiger are *A Brighter Sun* (1952) and *Turn Again Tiger* (1958). The first describes the developing inner conflicts in the teenage peasant Tiger. The second depicts Tiger wrestling with his demons and coming to a partial resolution of them. The experience of marginalization profoundly affects Tiger's psyche. Neither white nor Creole, the typical Asian immigrant strives to comprehend and to define his/her identity in North America.

This study does not analyze *The Plains of Caroni* (1970), in which the author revisits the Indo-Trinidadian peasants' world of the Tiger novels through Balgobin, the father, and Romesh, the son. Many of the issues of life among the cane workers are the same in the Tiger novels and *The Plains of Caroni*. Salick has compared the latter novel to Hemingway's *The Old Man and the Sea*, describing it as "the culmination of Selvon's cane narrative" (*The Novels of Samuel Selvon* 56). The exclusion of the novel from this study relates to the selective focus of the study on questions of identity, self-division, and self-discovery in the fictional works chosen for analysis rather than on surveying all examples of fiction by the authors discussed.

Selvon's Tiger is not only a South Asian, but also a West Indian under colonial British rule. The novel deals with "Tiger's questions and anxieties about the need for national independence and identity" (Barratt 108). As Barratt explains further,

> Put another way, Tiger seems to be aiming for a West Indian identity that would not assimilate, but incorporate, his Indian being. Tiger's relatives are products of the diaspora, displaced in a disconcertingly pluralistic society; and they are ferociously Hindu....

2. Identity and the Indo-Caribbean Experience

Tiger has been spawned by this threatened Hindu world; but he is also palpably West Indian. He is indeed an early West Indian hero whose quest for integrity and personal independence is a reflection of the individual's desire to overcome the colonial neglect so deeply embedded in the West Indian psyche ["Sam Selvon's Tiger" 109].

As in his London fiction, Selvon experiments with the Trinidadian dialect in *A Brighter Sun* (1952) in order to give immediacy to setting and characterization. According to Harold Barratt, Selvon developed the character of Tiger from his acquaintance with an old Indian of the same name (106). Barratt writes of the importance of *A Brighter Sun* because of the novel's emphasis on the evils of the colonial past such as "the psychic scars of slavery and the equally dehumanizing indenture system" ["Sam Selvon's Tiger" 106].

In this novel, Tiger is married early to the equally young and inexperienced Urmilla. Leaving the security of the community of Indian indentured workers in the sugarcane fields of Chaguanas, Tiger and Urmilla seek to build a life in Barataria, just outside the large city of Port of Spain, Trinidad's capital. Tiger has a difficult time trying to establish his manhood even to himself and he wishes that he had his father or an uncle present to turn to as a role model. Barratt aptly describes Tiger's self-realization: "Tiger learns from experience that manhood does not mean possessing a wife and fathering a child: nor does it mean smoking and drinking rum. Manhood means awareness of one's own identity as a unique individual; it also means satisfying one's hunger for knowledge" [107].

His parents are shocked by Tiger's socialization outside the Indian community in the racially mixed community of Barataria where Tiger builds a house. Tiger's parents are particularly uneasy about the young couple's friendship with their black neighbors Joe and Rita. Tiger remains divided between the traditionalist and macho upbringing and his new assimilationist inclinations. Several specific episodes indicate his self-division. The sales clerk in a fashionable store in Port of Spain ignores him and waits on a white woman. Tiger discovers that for colonial West Indians, for whom whiteness signals superiority, black and Indian are similarly marginalized, a concept which challenges his Indian upbringing. However, when he tries to get a doctor for Urmilla during a severe storm, the black and Asian doctors are rude. An English doctor from Port of Spain comes to help. Tiger learns that there is good and evil in every race, and that all people are the same. In yet another episode, his macho Indian peasant upbringing surfaces when he beats the pregnant Urmilla for wearing makeup and accepting a drink from the Americans who have come to dinner at their house. Rum-drinking is another aspect of his macho Indian peasant persona. He turns to drink as he ponders the problems of human existence, especially his own.

Tiger's conversations with his neighbor Joe indicate his growing anxiety about his sense of self. Barratt sums up Tiger's preoccupation as a quest to balance his Creolization with his Indianness (109). Tiger's quest for self continues in *Turn Again Tiger* (1958), the sequel to *A Brighter Sun*. Tiger's peasant upbringing and his closeness to the land are recurring motifs in both novels. In the sequel, Tiger returns to the land. In the earlier novel, Tiger copes with stress by contemplating the land that he cultivates. Seeking solace in the land or in nature, Tiger reaffirms his peasant roots. Barratt suggests that

> These moments of communion with the land demonstrate Tiger's abiding love and respect for a power he does not fully comprehend but of which he is nonetheless fully cognizant. Wordsworth and Coleridge, one feels, would have understood Tiger's oneness with land, sky, and sun. Union with the land, furthermore, gives Tiger the solace he needs and the strength to persevere ["Sam Selvon's Tiger" 110].

In *A Brighter Sun*, Tiger leaves farming to make some money working with Americans who are building a road through Barataria. In *Turn Again Tiger*, Tiger returns to farming to help his father, who becomes the foreman of an experimental cane plantation run by Robinson, an Englishman. Tiger's conflicts and his dilemmas about his sense of identity climax in his wordless single sexual encounter with Robinson's wife, Doreen:

> She took a step forward, another. She was close to him. He held the cutlass tightly and said to himself that he would kill her. When he said that, it gave him courage: his grip tightened and he felt that if he killed her everything would be all right after [*Turn Again Tiger* 177].

Tiger's encounter with Doreen is a symbolic death. It is the death of the youthful Tiger who is divided within himself. A new Tiger emerges as he gives up his drinking habits and is more at peace with himself in his world.

Turn Again Tiger systematically traces the central character's attempts to comprehend the meaning of his life, the confusion of historical, cultural, psychological, sociological messages that constitute his Trinidadian predicament. Sitting under a poui tree, Tiger

> remembered his early years in Chaguanas. In those days he never

thought about what he did. He tried now to follow the pattern that had led him to the hill, the experience of his marriage, of having a child, of growing up in the village of Barataria away from the influence of his parents. All his life spread out before him, and he sought the purpose. All his life had led to this indecision on the hill, looking down into a dark valley [*Turn Again Tiger* 6].

Roydon Salick comments that "Tiger is Selvon's epic hero who must found a politically independent, racially integrated Trinidad, and who must fashion an idiom supple enough to absorb and express creolized experience" (*The Novels of Samuel Selvon* 34). Tiger tries to make sense of the recurring phenomena of peasant life in Trinidad:

There was one thing he must do soon: he must come to grips with his life, understand the possibilities and reconcile himself to the limit of opportunity. Whichever way he looked at it, there was no denying that here was life being lived, in the island, in the valley, in the cane fields. Whatever dissatisfaction he felt made no difference to the acts of living carried on day after day by the people he knew: the eating, the sleeping, the working, the laughter and the drink in the evening.... Each man was occupied in a little world of his own, unconcerned with the rest [*Turn Again Tiger* 135].

For a peasant, Tiger is unusually perceptive and well read. His education intensifies his dilemma:

He went outside and he brought out all the books he had, and he sat on the steps with them and crumpled all the pages. He threw them in a heap on the ground in front of him and set fire to the paper. 'No more books', he told himself, watching them burn, 'they only make me miserable. Plato, Aristotle, Shakespeare, the lot. All them fellars dead and gone, and they ain't help me to solve nothing.' [*Turn Again Tiger* 136].

Salick views the burning of the books as an example of Tiger's "confusion and emotional turmoil" (34). The illicit sexual encounter with Doreen, the fight between Tiger and Babolal, and Tiger's book burning are all episodes symbolic of inner confusion and conflict. Salick points out that the other characters in *Turn Again Tiger* are also in the process of confronting change and the resulting confusion, tracing inner journeys towards maturation (41).

Tiger's wife Urmilla is a case in point of a character that grows from adolescence to adulthood and responsibility. Despite the love and devotion of his young wife, Tiger keeps his dilemmas to himself. Urmilla's journey of maturation is within the realm of a traditional marriage and domesticity. Her life is full of household chores and her dilemmas are seemingly more simple than his; for example, trying to keep her best white shoes clean:

> Urmilla had on her best sari and a pair of high-heel shoes, and she tried to walk elegantly. The shoes were lily-white when she left home, but walking to the main road from Five Rivers they had gathered wisps of dry grass and mud stains [*Turn Again Tiger* 160].

Even as Tiger has his violent and illicit sexual encounter with Doreen, Urmilla is expecting their second child. In the world of the Trinidadian Hindu farmer, men and women appear to live in different worlds. Ultimately, as Tiger reconciles his inner conflicts, he also gives up drinking and becomes more conscious of his duties to his family. He is more accepting of his life's burdens and the confusing, multiracial society of Trinidad. The acceptance of difference becomes symbolic of maturation in Selvon's Tiger.

3

Self-Definition and Difference: Ved Mehta and Ruth Prawer Jhabvala

Voices, characters, and themes exploring issues of self-definition and difference with regard to South Asians have continued to appear in *The New Yorker* since the nineteen fifties. Outstanding contributors in the best *New Yorker* tradition are Ved Mehta, one of the magazine's staff writers in his early career, and celebrated screenwriter Ruth Prawer Jhabvala. While Mehta moved from India to the U.S. in his early life, Jhabvala relocated to India in 1951, having married an Indian (Parsi) architect. Mehta's narratives explore the bicultural experience of South Asians in America while Jhabvala's most successful fictions recreate the conflicting emotions as well as the behaviors of Europeans moving into South Asian society. Ved Mehta favors autobiography, which nonetheless draws heavily upon nonrealistic techniques. Jhabvala's fiction excels in psychological exploration of the self-division and conflicting passions of European-born women who fall in love with Indian men and their land of contradictions. Both writers create strong-willed female characters. However, Jhabvala's characters usually turn out to be less than heroic in their actions and discoveries.

Ved Mehta's bicultural autobiographical narratives present an essential paradox in that Mehta, blind from early childhood, provides vividly descriptive accounts of the Asian American quest for self-definition. Mehta's insights into the Asian American search for identity have unusual intensity. Paradoxically, Mehta "sees" more deeply than those with sight. His prose contains an almost poetic sensibility in his heightened awareness of sensory perceptions. Mehta unifies his lengthy prose narratives by developing the theme of "on his blindness." The influence of British fiction writers is significant in Mehta's prose. In seeking to define his bicultural identity between India and America, and between sight and blindness, Mehta emphasizes the difficult transition for a first-generation immigrant. The critical evaluation of Mehta's autobiography amidst works of prose fiction presents challenges in defining genre, characterization, and the use of language.

Autobiography such as Ved Mehta's clearly borrows heavily from fictional techniques, to the extent that the reader is left puzzling over what is fictional and what is factual and authentic, since Mehta's self-exploration goes back to his early childhood. Mehta's art presents an achievement comparable with that of Helen Keller's writings. He is a South Asian American writer who frequently reworks his Old World texts into New World contexts, thereby bringing to life the thoughts and feelings of the first-generation immigrant from India. An essential paradox emerges in Mehta's bicultural autobiographical narratives. Mehta's definitions of his Asian American experience provide insights of unusual intensity.

Ved Parkash Mehta was born in India in 1934. He has been a staff writer for *The New Yorker* since the early 1960s. He went blind from meningitis at the age of three. His father sent him to the Arkansas State School for the Blind when he was fifteen. He attended Pomona College in California. Then Mehta returned to India and went on to Balliol College at Oxford University. His first book was *Face to Face* (1957), which received widespread critical acclaim. Then came *Walking the Indian Streets* (1960). Several autobiographical works followed. *Daddyji* (1972) describes his father's life, personality, and habits; *Mamaji* focuses on his mother. Mehta describes his life at a Bombay school for the blind in *Vedi* (1982), and his return home in *The Ledge Between the Streams* (1984). His only novel, *Delinquent Chacha* (1967), is about an elderly and eccentric Indian. He wrote a film script, *Chachaji, My Poor Relation*, based on this novel. *The Photographs of Chachaji* (1980) is about the filming of *Chachaji* for British television. *Sound-Shadows of the New World* (1985) contains his memories of his college days in California.

Mehta has also written about political subjects. His insightful accounts contain both humor and warmth. However, his political works have elicited a mixed response from critics. These writings on political subjects include *Fly and the Fly-Bottle: Encounters with British Intellectuals* (1963), *The New Theologian* (1966), *Portrait of India* (1970), *Mahatma Gandhi and His Apostles* (1977), *The New India* (1978), and *A Family Affair: India under Three Prime Ministers* (1982). Altogether Ved Mehta has written twenty-one books over forty years.

Mehta's conversations with leading British philosophers and historians appeared in *Fly and the Fly-Bottle* (1963). This book received fairly positive responses in Britain such as David Caute's comment that

> Mehta has interviewed a considerable number of eminent philosophers and historians, and if it has proved beyond his range (and

3. Self-Definition and Difference   31

whose range is it not beyond?) to read all their works, he has at least fashioned a series of workable syntheses out of second-hand opinions and casual gossip....

Yet he is a phenomenally quick and acute observer, marvelously adept at grasping and conveying the essence of a personality as it may appear in the first twenty minutes of a direct confrontation. As for those heroes who are now dead (Wittgenstein, Namier, Tawney), one can only admire his subtle use of varied reminiscences, his ability to suggest the shape and weight of the gravestone supporting the multi-colored wreaths ["Mehta" 289].

Mehta is kinder to the philosophers than the historians in this book. The *New Theologian* (1966) contains three groups of interviews, recorded in his lively style, with theologians in the United States, England, and Germany. Mehta is a skilled interviewer. Anthony Kenny provides a fair assessment when he writes that "The records of the interviews are enlivened by the author's unique talent for reproducing idiosyncrasies of speech rhythm"(290).

The interview treatment seems to be fairest when dealing with those writers whose reputations are based mainly on pamphlets or television interviews; it seems extremely unfair to serious scholars like Barth and Bultman. In this book perhaps the fairest and fullest account is contained in the biography of Bonhoeffer; the method is seen at its worst in the treatment of Reinhold Niebuhr. We are given an account of a brief conversation in which Niebuhr criticized Tillich for other-worldliness. But most of what is said about Niebuhr consists of trivial details.

Portrait of India (1970) attempts the near-impossible task of describing the somewhat unusual and entirely non–Western conditions of living in India. Written in the best traditions of American journalism, this book is remarkable for its flowing prose. Reviewer Bernard Nossiter comments that

In the best *New Yorker* tradition, he adopts a neutral stance. His *Portrait*, really an impressionist arrangement of brush strokes, loosely strings together the disparate accounts he wrote for the magazine. It is as deliberately formless and themeless as the complex subcontinent ["Mehta" 291].

Yet other critics such as Mervyn Jones point out that Mehta ignores rural India:

As for the content, the immense vacancy in the book is that it tells us nothing about the India where 80 percent of the people live—

rural India. As we are led from Delhi to Bombay to Calcutta to Madras, we must ask how anyone can spend many months in a country without placing the emphasis where it so manifestly belongs ["Mehta" 291].

Ved Mehta's own expatriate sensibilities and his early life in an upper-middle-class Indian home contribute to an avoidance of India's extreme oppositions — urban life vs. rural life, affluence and education vs. hunger, illiteracy, and abject misery. While his political works on India contain serious research, they still come from the viewpoint of a Westernized upper-middle-class visitor.

In *Mahatma and His Apostles* (1977), Mehta quotes from his interviews with Gandhi's disciples. According to Leonard A. Gordon, "The small contribution of this book is in the quotations from the disciples. From these the flesh-and-blood Gandhi, particularly the personal man, steps forth. We hear anew of Gandhi's experiments with food, sexual discipline, and basic hygiene" ("Mehta" 292).

Mehta's *The New India* (1978) attempts to describe the oppressive regime of the late Indian Prime Minister Indira Gandhi from June 26, 1975, to March 21, 1977. Pam Jablons finds Mehta's political research to be vast but his analysis to be somewhat deficient ("Mehta" 293).

A Family Affair: India Under Three Prime Ministers (1982) is also flawed in its lack of deeper analysis. Robert L. Hardgrave, Jr., comments that

> Despite Mehta's serious purpose, he rarely cuts below the surface of personality or politics. Much of the book is a chronicle of rumors and allegations emanating from New Delhi, a report of the fads, idiosyncrasies, and machinations of the "celibate Janata leaders." This is not without interest, but it provides little real understanding of the political and social forces shaping Indian political life ["Mehta" 296].

Earlier and later reviews and recent British and American criticism of Mehta's autobiographical works praise the vivid detail of his descriptions. Mehta's prose becomes his form of vision as he locates himself in the center of his lengthy and vivid autobiographical narratives. He is appropriately as concerned about the characters and settings as about his own evolving bicultural perceptions of self and identity.

In *Face to Face* (1957), Mehta explores his return to India after being educated in the U.S. and England. Memories of his Indian upbringing and the powerful influence of his physician father dominate this book. Returning to India, he questions the age-old fatalism predominant in his parent culture. All handicaps are negligible when placed against the tremendous

3. Self-Definition and Difference

obstacle of correcting the attitude that looks upon blindness as a punishment inflicted by the gods for a sin committed in the previous incarnation. He feels that his love and devotion for his native land will not be enough to keep him permanently in an environment where he is denied opportunities because of his blindness (*Face to Face* 365).

In describing these early experiences, Mehta clearly places himself in the Western tradition of writing, emphasizing his lifelong interest in history, philosophy, and poetry. There is immediacy in Mehta's use of language when he remembers how the world of sight was lost to him in childhood:

> If my age and the length of the sickness deprived me of the treasured memories of sight, they also reduced things which are valued so much in the sighted world to nothing more than mere words, empty of meaning. I started living in a universe where it was not the flood of sunshine streaming in through the nursery window or the color of a rainbow, a sunset or full moon that mattered, but the feel of the sun against the skin, the slow drizzling sound of the spattering rain, the feel of the air just before the coming of the quiet night, the smell of the stubble grass on a warm morning. It was a universe where at first—but only at first–I made my way fumbling and faltering [*Face to Face* 3–4].

Around the time of his graduation from Pomona College, he is warned of the conditions for the blind in India by the Indian ambassador, who is visiting Los Angeles. The ambassador tells him that he would be ineligible for both the civil and the diplomatic services of the Indian government because of his blindness (*Face to Face* 364).

In *Face to Face*, he remembers his father's method of explaining true understanding in love and marriage as being dependent upon understanding each other's problems (104). Mehta's Western-educated father comments on the difference between the Asian practice of arranging a marriage where love is expected to grow, and the modern-day Western expectation that love should be a prerequisite to marriage: "Love grows gradually. This is the tradition of our society, and these are the means we have adopted to make our marriage successful and beautiful" (107).

Mehta's father explains to him that as a blind young man in India he could not expect to find a compatible spouse:

> "Oh, you could get married in India all right, but not well, not happily, because the kind of girl you would want could not be found here.... India is a harsh land. Marriage here is like a business transaction and people weigh and measure their liabilities and assets

> carefully. In the States, no doubt your blindness would make a marriage difficult, though I believe not impossible, because there values are different and marriage is made by the two people involved without the agency of parents. But all this you will only find out by living there" [*Face to Face* 221].

Mehta thus suggests that his early relationships with American women came about because of his difference from other Indian men of his generation—his blindness.

Mehta describes his love of American classical music and books that various American student friends helped him to discover:

> As I prepare to leave for England, I am surrounded by cartons full of books and records, two vices to which I have given great play in the last seven years. Each familiar cover of a book encloses not only a fund of knowledge, but a fond memory of the readers whose tireless efforts made these books come alive for me. The great history of Thucydides conjures up Ann; Goethe and Joyce, Albert; Plato and T.S. Eliot, Eugene. The records have their similar associations. The album of *Don Giovanni* brings the image of Dick, beside me in the auditorium; and Bach's B-minor Mass, JoAn [*Face to Face* 365].

Face to Face is one of the earliest works by a South Asian American. The different perspective emerging in Mehta's writing was observed by an early reviewer:

> The American section follows and is difficult to describe. No other foreigner has written about the United States in quite this style. There is neither eulogy nor denunciation in it. The Arkansas school was poorly equipped and understaffed. Life was far from luxurious and instruction was not always of the best. Fanaticism, racial and religious, intruded once or twice. All this Mehta noted and set down precisely. He closes that episode without any extravagance of any kind. But one thing they did have — excellent instructors to teach the blind how to move about confidently. So there he was liberated, physically and mentally, and there is no doubt that he knows that [Johnson 288].

Although *Face to Face* was an instant success, *Walking the Indian Streets* (1960) was less kindly received. The detailing that is one of Mehta's greatest assets as a writer came up for criticism from skeptical reviewers:

> Ved Mehta handicaps himself doubly in *Walking the Indian Streets*. He cannot help his blindness and has, indeed, turned it by a mir-

3. Self-Definition and Difference 35

acle of will power and courage into something resembling an asset, but he could not hope to write a book about India as if he were not blind [Matthews 288].

Mehta identifies very early on with his western-educated father's philosophy of life. His questioning of Indian superstitions is gentle and amusing, as he recognizes that superstitious beliefs provided an emotional support system for his mother—whom the author loves and seems to understand in *Mamaji* (1974), his third volume of autobiography. Mehta writes:

> That night, fearing that Daddyji's remark about the horoscope might bring the evil eye upon Om or upon the family, she took a handful of red chilis and circled them in the air over Om's cot, and then, before going to sleep, she prayed to Ganesh not to punish Daddyji for his insult or send her more afflictions. But soon afterward she was confined to bed with a low grade fever and a persistent cough, which she secretly attributed to the evil eye [287].

The depiction of his mother in *Mamaji* is similar to his characterization of her in *Face to Face*, where Mehta describes her application of painful remedies obtained from herbalists (*hakims*) to restore his sight, and his physician father's anger:

> One night when my mother was administering these eye drops, and I was protesting with loud cries, my father unexpectedly returned. He asked and I told him why I was crying. He was outraged [6].

Even after Mehta's father condemns the Indian folk remedies, Mehta recalls that his mother would occasionally use them on him till he was about eleven (*Face to Face* 7). His mother's continuing faith in folk remedies is clearly indicative of her strong-willed personality.

While *Face to Face* has a few sketches of his mother's behavior, *Mamaji* chronicles the full-length story of a woman who seeks to be a devoted wife and a good mother despite her ignorance resulting from the lack of a formal education. In several ways, Mamaji is similar to the strong-willed South Asian women characters created by Jhabvala.

Vedi (1982) has an almost Dickensian quality as Mehta describes the terrible living conditions of the boy's dormitory in the charitable blind school in Bombay:

> Whatever progress I made, I never got used to the boys' common bathroom. It smelled so bad that I had to hold my nose when I

was there. The floor was wet, and sometimes, if I wasn't careful, I would slip and fall. Wasps seemed to always be buzzing around the walls; I remember once I got too close to a corner, and a wasp stung me.

Deoji had told me about a bathroom ghost who lived inside the wall. "If anyone stays here too long, the bathroom ghost will pounce on him and bite off his nose," he had said. "If he ever attacks you, just pray to Jesus, Mary, and Joseph" [35].

For once, the real fears of people who cannot see is recorded in this text as Mehta recounts the cruelty of the sinister Sighted Master, who silences the crying boys Jaisingh and Ramesh:

One night, both Ramesh and Jaisingh began crying, and neither would stop. I heard the Sighted Master curse and get up. I waited for the scraping sound that I always heard when he was scraping around for his shoe, but I didn't hear it. "The blind devils!" he muttered. "I would rather break stones, but there are no jobs to be had. The damned blind devils." He stubbed his toe on the foot of my long bed and cursed some more. I heard him walk slowly, in his bare feet, to Jaisingh's bed. "I will finish Ras Mohun's Helen Keller," he said [Vedi 198].

Neither the author nor the other boys really know how the boys disappeared from the dormitory, but they fear the worst. Their fears emerge in rumor: "He killed them last night," Abdul said. "Both of them. The Sighted Master did, with two blows of a plank" [Vedi 199].

In Vedi, Mehta experiences an inner self-division as a rich boy in a school for orphans. He eats with the principal's family but his heart is with the poor boys at the dormitory. As anti-fungal drugs were not available in India, he recalls the burning of his hair with X-rays by his doctor to cure ringworm.

The transitions from the Bombay blind school to an Arkansas blind school and to Pomona College in California mark the writer's continuing search to define himself as a bicultural Asian American. In *Sound-Shadows of the New World* (1985), he recalls an encounter with racism:

"You ain't white, you know," Wayne said after a while.

"My people are not dark-skinned, like the Dravidians, in South India," I said. "We're fair-skinned Aryans — we come from the North."

"I don't know about all that. Here you're just white or not white, and I can see that you ain't white. You can't fool me" [*Sound-Shadows* 43].

3. Self-Definition and Difference

The young Mehta is unable to figure out where the Asian stands in the biracial society of the southern United States in the nineteen fifties:

> I wondered how dark I was, how much I looked like a Negro, and what my kinship with the Negro was — where I fitted into the social puzzle. I wanted somehow or the other to find out where I stood in the shading from white to black, to connect myself to the rest of the world. I ached to see, even for just a moment [*Sound-Shadows* 74].

Elsewhere, his experience of the Arkansas blind school is more positive when the principal, Mr. Woolly, arranges a surprise birthday celebration [*Sound Shadows* 214].

Reticent and shy, the teenaged Mehta tries to fit into the social life of an American college. In *The Stolen Light* (1989) he remembers an early infatuation:

> In the years that Johnnie and I were in college together, I never stopped thinking about her—almost to the exclusion of everybody else. Whenever I read a novel, I saw her as its heroine—most of all as Catherine Earnshaw [*Stolen Light* 6].

The influence of Victorian fiction may be easily inferred from the allusion to Emily Brontë. Mehta describes a more intense relationship with a date whom he names Mary:

> The moment of reckoning had passed, and I sighed with relief. She took my face in her hands. "You can tell everything. I bet you even know how I look on a particular day." "Sometimes."
> "Then the blind can see. God has his own mysterious ways of compensating for everything."
> The focus had shifted from my abilities to these of the blind generally. And when it came to them, I was as brutally honest as though I were not one of them. "They can do nothing of the kind," I said [*Stolen Light* 443].

Familiar use of the vague pronouns "them" and "they" Americanize his South Asian voice and he seems to unconsciously rethink the words of his father Daddyji while confronting Mary's superstitious belief. Mehta's seeing is not physical, it is a hypothetical sense perception of settings, characters, and episodes described in his autobiographical writings.

In trying to define his bicultural identities between America and India, and between sight and blindness, Mehta exhibits an almost Keatsian "negative capability" which universalizes his experiences for his international reading public.

> Dealing with the public on the street was no easier. As I was threading my way through traffic on a wide street, calculating my distance from the oncoming cars or running through a gap in the line of cars, a stranger would bellow "Watch out!" and I would freeze to the spot, thinking that a car was about to run me down, or that I was about to crash into a perilous obstacle, or that the street was dug up and I was about to fall into a trench and crack my head open, just as Mr. Hartman had always predicted....
>
> I felt that meddlesome strangers had dogged me from my childhood. When I was growing up, it seemed that people who didn't know me were always trying to give me a hand, often making me lose my balance and fall. If I screamed with rage, I would be scolded by one family member or another for not knowing how to accept help gracefully, and so contributing to my fall. Now, in the street, the stranger whose help had been spurned would fire a parting shot like "Then *get* run over!" [*Sound-Shadows* 192–193].

Elsewhere, he describes his own social and cultural heritage to a young woman he is dating. He tells her that she does not know his family or his Indian native language—Punjabi (*Sound-Shadows* 328). He also thinks that she would not receive his parents' approval and fit in the parameters of nationality, ethnicity, and caste that defined Mehta's cultural roots (*Sound-Shadows* 328).

Even as a teenager, Mehta was keenly aware of the tension between Old World and New World social practices that has subsequently become a recurring motif in Asian American literature. He undergoes a masculine rite of passage that makes him aware of the complex nature of human sexuality. His first sexual encounter with a young woman, named Phyllis, takes on an unexpectedly complicated dimension when she tells him that she is pregnant (*The Stolen Light* 291). Later, when she has an abortion, he learns that the child was not his. Although he feels sorry for her, he firmly resolves not to see her again.

The contrast between East and West acquires a different perspective in *Delinquent Chacha* (1967), where Mehta attempts to develop a comic Anglophile Indian in the larger context of the transition from colonial India to the modern Indian republic. Mehta opens the novel in India, but immediately moves the setting to England. The novel's flaws are listed by John Wain, who writes: "Delinquent Chacha, with his worship of everything English and his romantic obsession with "Ox-Ford," is absurd, but he is absurd in a vacuum; there is no firm position, either Eastern or Western, against which his flutterings are silhouetted" ("Mehta" 290).

3. Self-Definition and Difference

Throughout Mehta's childhood and youth, his westernized father is a powerful influence in shaping his thoughts and values. *Daddyji* (1972) is his short book about his father's family history, early life, education, marriage, the birth of children, Mehta's blindness—all set during the early years of India's freedom movement. According to reviewer Paul Scott: "Conceived as a series of cameos of village and urban family life from the end of the last century to the end of the first 40 years of this, *Daddyji*, intimate, personal, is as well a history of modern India in the making" (292).

In *The Ledge Between the Streams* (1984), another volume of familial autobiography, Mehta is about fifteen. He is in transition between the blind school in Bombay and preparations to attend school in Arkansas in the U.S. Once again, Mehta shows his constant awareness of overriding issues in South Asian history and politics. One of Mehta's most chilling descriptions is of an interview with a Sikh refugee who had survived a Muslim attack on his community:

> "Your hands—what happened?"
> "In a temple. Sahib. We had taken refuge there with our families. We had been sleeping there for four nights. The fifth night, they came. We expected them. We were ready for them. They told us to come out and become converts. They swore that it was not a trick to disarm us and rape and torture our wives and daughters. They said, 'As Allah is our witness, a mullah is standing outside to perform the ceremony. If you become converts, you can go back to your homes. No one will trouble you.' We cried, 'We would rather die than become filthy Muslims!' We set upon them like a pride of lions.... We started killing our women to save them from torture and rape. I cut the throat of my daughter with one stroke. It was the turn of my wife. I hesitated, and I was overpowered by a defiler. I fought back. I think I killed him, but a whole group of them came at me and chopped off my hands and cut off my ears" [*The Ledge* 409–410].

Mehta is a skilled interviewer. In a brief sketch, he brings to life the horrors of religious fanaticism and communal riots in the Indian subcontinent. The sketch reminds readers of a monumental event in the history of modern South Asia which Asian historians term "Partition," aptly summed up by Niaz Zaman in the following passage:

> It included the largest single migration of history, involving a total of eleven and a half million people, ten and a half crossing the border of the Punjab—Hindus and Sikhs moving eastward, Muslims westwards—and another million crossing the borders of Ben-

gal—Hindus moving west, Muslims moving east. Along with the misery of that movement were the riots and conflagrations, an outpouring of savagery unprecedented in its scale and span. Estimates of deaths range from half a million to two million [*A Divided Legacy* 3].

However, Mehta's greatest emphasis remains on the closeness of South Asian family bonds. Another vivid recollection is of his preparations for leaving his family in India: "Mamaji busied herself in getting my clothes sewn. Sister Umi started knitting me a sweater. Sister Nimi bought me records of love songs of Saigal and Noor Jehan to remind me of home" (*The Ledge* 516).

As his preparations for America intensify, his father arranges for Mehta to meet with the Indian Prime Minister, Jawaharlal Nehru, a legendary figure in the history of modern India. Mehta remembers that he was the first blind Indian boy to go to America for his education (*The Ledge* 515–517).

This actual encounter with Nehru is memorable because of Nehru's message itself:

> Prime Minister Nehru seemed to be lost in thought, but then he dictated this slowly, as if he were thinking it out as he went along: "I shall be an unofficial ambassador of my country. Wherever I go, I will behave in a manner that will bring honor to my homeland."
> I took out the page and handed it to him. The cheep-cheep of a sparrow on the veranda sounded very loud in the silence.
> "Panditji, would you autograph it?" Daddyji said.
> "Oh!" he exclaimed. "Oh! If you like."
> Daddyji gave Pandit Nehru his fountain pen, and he signed it [*The Ledge* 518].

In a sense, Nehru's writing underlies much of Mehta's writing, which repeatedly presents the familiar style of life of ordinary Indian people with warmth, humor, deep insight, and compassion. Back and forth between East and West in his education and travels, Mehta is realistic in depicting the positive and negative aspects of daily life in both cultural contexts.

Continents of Exile: All for Love (2001) is Ved Mehta's most recent autobiographical narrative and perhaps the most intensely personal one. It compares in intensity with his early accounts of blindness. In this novelistic autobiographical volume Mehta describes all his failed love affairs, culminating in how he ended up in psychotherapy in New York in the nineteen sixties. This daring book is quite different from Mehta's earlier style in that each episode contains action in addition to Mehta's vivid descriptions. This work is largely a New World narrative in setting but the core of the text is a universal human problem—that of a disabled person who longs for a normal romantic relationship. In many ways this book reflects upon the advice on love and marriage offered to Mehta by his father when he left for America as a young man. In this volume Mehta spares his readers neither the details of his failed relationships nor the sense of loss, defeat, and failure. The dedication of the book is to Mehta's wife Linn, a subtle suggestion that the author is healed of his past.

The book is structured as four episodes with four women who love Mehta but leave him for sighted men. The first rejection is from the Jewish ballet dancer Judith, of whom the book contains a photograph. Judith has a relationship with Mehta while he is beginning his career at *The New Yorker*. Judith leaves Mehta suddenly for her old Jewish boyfriend, whom she marries. The reason she gives is that her parents had expectations that she would choose a Jewish husband. Mehta even describes the phase of impotence he suffers during his liaison with Judith.

The author's next relationship begins after Judith's departure from Mehta's life. This is with the Englishwoman Vanessa, who is temporarily resident in New York. He makes the mistake of taking her love for granted. He travels abroad for his writing assignments. Vanessa finds another man to love.

The third relationship develops with Lola, the writer's beautiful young Eurasian secretary, whom he falls in love with on a writing assignment in India. This woman earns the approval of his parents. He arranges for her to come to America where she lives with him briefly. While Mehta contemplates a permanent relationship, Lola leaves for England to join her less educated, working-class boyfriend there. She eventually marries this boyfriend. The Lola episode is illustrative of a nineteen-sixties style of life where men and woman seem to hop in and out of one another's beds without making commitments. Lola first aborts her boyfriend's baby because she wants to be with Mehta. Then she aborts Mehta's baby after she decides to leave Mehta and marry her boyfriend. As a sensitive artist, Mehta suffers emotionally with Lola, with whom he had hoped for a permanent relationship.

Mehta's fourth failed love affair is with an American woman named Kilty, who also continues her relations with her old boyfriend while she is seeing Mehta. Kilty leaves New York to attend Yale University in New Haven, Connecticut, as a full-time doctoral student. Also, Kilty of the unaccountable behaviors enters deep psychotherapy.

While with Kilty, Mehta himself almost has a nervous breakdown. He enters psychotherapy with a Dr. Bak, who explains that Mehta desired women who were visually beautiful and desired by other men. Bak reasoned that these attractive women were not able to commit to Mehta because they needed reassurance from their partners that they were valued for their visual beauty. Hence they left Mehta for those sighted men whom Mehta adjudged to be inferiors. Bak puts Mehta face to face with his own lack of perception regarding his own flaws in his relationships. For a while the psychiatrist is a very important figure in Mehta's life, yet Mehta never really knows Bak well enough. Only when the psychiatrist dies suddenly does Mehta learn that he had been ill for a long time.

Finally, Mehta concludes that as a writer he was permanently influenced by being in psychoanalysis (345). Mehta states that he did not get married for thirteen years after he started treatment with Bak (345). He also ascribes his autobiographical works to the influences of psychotherapy:

> The truth is that I cannot imagine what my life would have been like without analysis; nor can I fathom what gains or losses, if any, came from it.... One thing I can say with some assurance is that, after I began analysis, I found myself able to write in a whole new autobiographical vein, exploring interior worlds previously inaccessible to me. Thus, since then, I have been writing a series of books, of which this is the ninth, that explore the boundaries of time and memory, the clash of culture and self, and the meaning of place and exile—as I have experienced them [*All for Love* 345].

In contrast to Mehta's warmth for the familial style of life of ordinary Indian people, Ruth Jhabvala targets her American and British audiences' perception of differences between East and West in her characterization, plot construction, and themes. Jhabvala's ordinary Indians and Europeans are mostly losers. The typecast character of Yiddish tradition, the *shlemiel*, the loser who is a sympathetic figure, appears in most of Jhabvala's fiction. In Jhabvala's South Asia, there are no heroes.

Born in Germany in 1927, Ruth Prawer Jhabvala is of Jewish heritage. She immigrated to England where she obtained a degree in English Literature from London University. After her transplantation into South Asian society in 1951, she has written nine novels and three collections of short stories, along with numerous screenplays. Although Jhabvala is not a South Asian by race, her themes and characters are South Asian. She has won numerous awards for her fiction set in South Asia, including Britain's Booker Prize in 1975 for *Heat and Dust*. The influence of British colonial literature on Jhabvala is evident as manifested in her award-winning screenplays of novels written by the Bloomsbury novelists of the early twentieth century.

Jhabvala's fiction has attracted considerable scholarly attention over

3. Self-Definition and Difference

time. Laurie Sucher ascribes her popularity with American audiences to her winning an award in 1984 from the MacArthur Foundation (*The Politics of Passion* 3). Ralph Crane states that during her twenty-five years living in India Jhabvala "emerged as a major novelist of contemporary India" (*Ruth Prawer Jhabvala* 9). Crane makes the valid observation that history and politics, particularly the themes of the British Raj and Partition, recur as a backdrop to Jhabvala's fiction (126). Crane also points out that

> Jhabvala's position as an outsider herself has always made her highly conscious of cultural differences and influences, and consequently her novels and stories always force the reader to be aware of and even confront the cultural influences and prejudices Jhabvala exposes ... at times focuses attention on the East-West encounter [*Ruth Prawer Jhabvala* 9].

Jhabvala's use of European women who form relationships with South Asian men continues the tradition set in E. M. Forster's *A Passage to India*. The South Asian male is frequently depicted as a sex object, and a lazy and lustful person. The main character of the short story titled "The Interview" is a case in point, a young married man who lives with his older brother presumably after having gone to many job interviews without being hired. In "The Interview," the first-person narrator leaves the building where he has a job interview because he does not really want a job. Although he is a married man, he revels in his erotic fantasies about his older brother's wife, who is one reason for his not wanting to find a job and move to a separate dwelling. He reflects:

> I don't think I would like to live away from my sister-in-law. I often look at her and it makes me happy. Even though she is not young anymore, and she is still beautiful. She is tall, with big hips and big breasts and eyes that flash; she often gets angry, and when she is angry, she is the most beautiful of all ["The Interview" 59].

The narrator has no sense of shame about his desires and behaviors. "It is true I have no job and no immediate prospect of getting one. It is true that I am dependent on my brother. Everyone knows that. There is no shame in it: there are many people without jobs" (66).

Over and over again, Jhabvala's European women characters confront their inner demons by having sex with South Asian men. Much negative stereotyping is attached to these South Asian lovers—the residue of the British Empire. Laurie Sucher traces the genealogy of Jhabvala's heroines to characters such as Lady Chatterley and Blanch duBois: the highborn lady who falls in love with a man who is her social inferior (28). Jhabvala's satiric portraits are in sharp contrast to the solid middle-class value system of the South Asian family structure depicted over and over again by Ved Mehta. As Jhabvala states in her introduction to *Out of India*, the love-hate relationship with India and its people has been a major formative influence in her own artistic career. Laurie Sucher comments that

> Jhabvala's fiction takes as a starting point the defiance of the racial and patriarchal taboo: not only do her wandering women exercise sexual freedom, but they do so with Indian men. But though their actions defy Western patriarchy, they invite loud disapproval from non-western patriarchal society as well (including women, of course) [*The Politics of Passion* 120].

As Jhabvala's fiction depicts only a margin and a fragment of the South Asian experience, a few fictional scenarios are analyzed for points of comparison to Mehta's much fuller canvas. In "Passion," the central character Betsy, a European woman living in India, starts the forbidden process of fraternizing with Indian males: "Once Manny kissed Betsy. It was entirely unexpected.... Waves of rapture passed over her like a fainting fit. But it seemed he was more collected than she was" ("Passion" 90). Betsy becomes aware of her own sexuality in this brief scene with her roommate's boyfriend, Manny. Soon she finds an Indian lover, a married man:

> He jumped on her in the same sudden way Manny had done. Betsy thought, do all Indian men make love like this? In spite of his frail appearance, Har Gopal was strong. Not with Manny's massive body strength, but he had a sort of sharp, incisive, relentless quality that rode down opposition. He went straight ahead without question, not skillful but resolute, steely. He commanded respect ["Passion" 94].

Betsy finds the relationship to be overpowering. She confides in her roommate Christine that she knows that the relationship seems to be improper because he is married with three children (95). But as the story's title suggests, the actions of the main characters are not entirely governed by reasoning.

Betsy soon incurs the disapproval of the expatriate European community. In a postcolonial Indian setting, Betsy, the descendant of colonials, becomes the subject of passion. She wants to live in India like an Indian but she is discouraged by her lover, who points out the reality of housing with a chronic shortage of running water and cockroach-infested homes as well as quarrelsome neighbors (103–104). The quarrel takes on a physical dimension as Har Gopal viciously pulls away from Betsy, swearing at her in Hindi. Manny comes to Betsy's assistance in dealing with her difficult Indian lover (104).

After Manny and Christine intervene in the fight between Har Gopal and Betsy, Har Gopal asks her to leave her friends. In her obedience and choice of an uncertain life in a foreign land, Betsy mirrors the contradiction of colonial dreams that had originally brought Europeans to India. She wants to live in a place "very cheap, very Indian" in a reminder of behavior that was described by European colonials as "going native"—almost a form of derangement. She also subordinates her individuality entirely to Har Gopal, who wants her to move away from Christine and Manny (104–105). Sucher suggests that Jhabvala's heroines tend to glorify the socially marginal men with whom they are in love (*The Politics of Passion* 27).

Like Betsy, Elizabeth in the short story "Two More Under the Indian Sun" is a transplant from Europe. Elizabeth, an English schoolteacher in her thirties, marries Raju, an Indian, and comes to live in Delhi, India. The philanthropist Margaret, the elderly widow of a British colonial officer, reminds Elizabeth of the active and pious English style of life which she has abandoned for the lazy ways of South Asia:

> Elizabeth was ashamed. The worst of it was she really had once been a serious person. She had been a schoolteacher in England, and devoted to her work and her children, on whom she spent far more time and above that, she had put in several evenings a week visiting old people who had no one to look after them. But all that had come to an end once she met Raju ["Two More Under the Indian Sun" 193].

Even the seemingly incorruptible widow Margaret is not impervious to the sexual attraction of Indian men:

> "Indian men have such marvelous eyes," Margaret said. "When they look at you, you can't help feeling all young and nice. But of course, your Raju thinks I'm just a fat, ugly old memsahib" ["Two More Under the Indian Sun" 197].

When Elizabeth refuses to accompany Margaret on a charitable bus trip with poor Tibetan orphans, Margaret is quite happy to turn her attention to Babaji, an elderly Indian friend who has taken to a spiritual life in the mountains:

> Margaret fussed over him. She stirred his tea and she arranged his

> shawl more securely over his shoulders.... She squeezed his knee in anticipatory joy, and he smiled at her and his thin old hand came down on top of her head in a gesture of affection or blessing ["Two More Under the Indian Sun" 198].

In her own pious fashion, Margaret too has embraced the ways of South Asia inclusive of her friendship with a South Asian man.

Jhabvala's satiric storytelling suggests that even "spiritual" encounters between the East and West can subtly turn into sexual occasions. Sucher suggests that in Jhabvala's stories of gurus and their disciples "European enthusiasm for spiritual quest and involvement with spiritual leaders is always uncomfortably close to feverish eroticism" (39). "How I Became a Holy Mother" is a first-person narrative by a twenty-three-year-old British model, Katie, who is in search of self in an ashram in South India. The story comically recounts Katie's misadventures:

> The door of my room was not the only one that was locked during those hot afternoons.... I felt there was something good and innocent about what they were doing. And after awhile—when we had told each other the story of our respective lives and had run out of conversation—Vishwa and I began to do it, too ["Holy Mother" 261].

Katie merely fits into the permissive atmosphere of the ashram: "One day there was an awful commotion outside. Master woke up as the Countess came in with two foreign disciples, a boy and a girl, who stood hanging their heads while she told us what she caught them doing" ("Holy Mother" 263).

Ultimately Katie is transformed into a fake holy mother, with posters of her embodying the Mother principle and of her lover Vishwa embodying the Guru—once again the South Asian male with the European female ("Holy Mother" 268). Such imagery suggests a reversal of the imagery of colonial times in the postcolonial setting where the South Asian male (formerly the colonized subject) becomes the dominant figure in his sexual domination of the European female.

The synthesis of all the motifs of these journeys of Europeans in the grip of love and hate amidst South Asia takes place in Jhabvala's much-acclaimed novel *Heat and Dust*. In it the narrator, an Englishwoman in her mid-twenties, travels to the small town of Satipur in India to research the story of her grandfather's first wife, Olivia, who had eloped with an Indian prince. Ralph Crane has compared this novel to Forster's *Passage to India* in its characterization and setting (*Ruth Prawer Jhabvala* 80–85):

3. Self-Definition and Difference

"Heat and dust become a metaphor for one India and for the effect that country has on Westerners" (86).

The novel is written in an epistolary style whereby Olivia's letters are juxtaposed with the narrator's modern-day letters. The epistolary structure establishes parallels between Olivia and the narrator. The first could not determine whether the child she was pregnant with was fathered by her English husband or the Nawab, the Indian prince who had become her lover; and the second has a relationship first with the Englishman Chid, who plays at becoming a Hindu holy man, then with her Indian landlord Inder Lal, whose wife is away. Like Olivia, who feels sympathetic to the Nawab partly because his wife has a mental illness, the narrator discerns that Inder Lal's wife, too, is mentally ill. Unlike Olivia, who had an illegal abortion and left the society of the British colonials permanently, the narrator, when she becomes pregnant, decides to have her baby and to stay on in the Indian mountain town where Olivia lived out her permanent exile. Looking at the snow on the Himalayan peaks, the narrator reflects, "Perhaps it is also what Olivia saw: the view—or vision—that filled her eyes all those years and suffused her soul" (*Heat and Dust* 180).

Olivia's abortion is arranged by the Nawab's mother, the Begum. It is not an experience with which, despite physical pain, she can engage fully as it represents a betrayal of her romantic dream. She is clad in a full Muslim veil (*burka*) and is escorted to the rickety old home of a midwife (*Heat and Dust* 166–167). The procedure is conducted under the supervision of the Begum (who presumably does not want a Eurasian grandchild):

> The midwife with the twig came towards her, holding it. Olivia understood that it was to be introduced into herself. The two women opened Olivia's legs and one of them held on to her ankles while the other pointed the twig. The Begum also bent over her to watch. Although the midwife worked swiftly and skillfully, the twig hurt Olivia as it entered into her. She was unable to stifle a cry. Then the Begum bent over her to look into her face and Olivia stared back at her. She *did* look like the Nawab, very much. She seemed as interested to study Olivia's face as Olivia was to study hers. For a moment they gazed into each other's eyes and then Olivia had to shut hers, as the pain below was repeated [*Heat and Dust* 168].

Jhabvala's narrative method may be encapsulated by applying Homi Bhabha's observation that "The enunciation of cultural difference problematizes the binary vision of past and present, tradition and modernity, at the level of cultural representation and its authoritative address" (*The Location of Culture* 35). Thus, in story after story, Jhabvala satirizes both

Europeans and South Asians, both groups undertaking everlasting and unresolved journeys to discover themselves. East meets West in Jhabvala's fiction as characters confront their fragmented psyches in the postmodern world.

4

The Immigrants' Search for Identity: Bharati Mukherjee and Chitra Banerjee Divakaruni

The South Asian immigrant's search for identity in America provides a common thread between the fiction of Bharati Mukherjee and Chitra Banerjee Divakaruni, both of whom are California-based writers and professors of creative writing. While Mukherjee's depiction of the failures and anxieties of her immigrant characters is satiric, Divakaruni's almost lyrical prose passages remind us that she is a poet who has turned to fiction. Both authors favor women's perspectives in their choice of characters and situations. While Mukherjee has carefully avoided feminist labels, Divakaruni is a well-known social crusader for the rights of South Asian women in abusive households.

The recurring theme in Bharati Mukherjee's fiction is the South Asian immigrants' search for identity amidst the alien culture of North America. Mukherjee's immigrants from South Asia encounter self-division, alienation, even madness as they seek to define themselves anew in their transition from the Old World to the New World. "Mukherjee's art of characterization depends heavily upon contrasting the public and private selves of her principal characters" (Pati 197). Mukherjee's diasporic South Asians encounter the "anarchy of the self" as they seek to reconcile their Old World paradigms of respecting traditions, of humility, of collective values, and of the renunciation of material desire with their New World pursuits of individualism and material success.

Mukherjee devotes greater efforts to the development of female characters than male characters (Pati 199). Her characterization incorporates both ethnic and gender stereotypes (Pati 199). Mukherjee's narrative method frequently employs satiric devices. According to Northrop Frye, "satire is irony which is structurally close to the comic: the comic struggle of two societies, one normal and the other absurd, is reflected in its double focus of morality and fantasy" (*Anatomy of Criticism* 224). Mukherjee's immigrants from South Asia, women and men, are mostly portrayed satirically. In her fiction, the South Asian immigrants' search for identity is largely a comic quest.

Bharati Mukherjee was born in Calcutta, India, on July 27, 1940. She attended a Catholic school along with her two sisters. In 1959, she received a B.A. from the University of Calcutta, followed by an M.A. from the University of Baroda in 1961 and an M.F.A. from the University of Iowa in 1963. In 1964, she married Canadian writer Clark Blaise. Mukherjee taught English at Marquette University and the University of Wisconsin-Madison from 1964 to 1965. She received her Ph.D. in English and Comparative Literature from the University of Iowa in 1969. She taught at McGill University, Montreal, Canada, from 1966 to 1980. In 1972, Mukherjee published *The Tiger's Daughter*. The novel *Wife* (1975) was a finalist for the Governor General's Award in Canada. Her *Days and Nights in Calcutta* (1977) was written in collaboration with husband, Clark Blaise. She received a Guggenheim Foundation Award in 1978.

Mukherjee emigrated to the U.S. in 1980 and embarked on a freelance teaching career at Skidmore College, Mountain State College, Queens College of CUNY, and Columbia University. She received the first prize from the Periodical Distributor's Association for her short story "Isolated Incidents." In 1981, she received the National Magazine Awards second prize for the essay "An Invisible Woman." From 1984 to 1987, she was an associate professor at Mountain State College in New Jersey. From 1984 to 1985, she was writer-in-residence at Emory University and she published *Darkness*. In 1986, Mukherjee held a National Endowment for the Arts grant. She became a full professor at the City University of New York in 1987. She published *The Sorrow and the Terror* with Clark Blaise in 1987. "The Tenant" was chosen for inclusion in *Best American Stories of 1987*. *The Middleman and Other Stories* appeared in 1988. She received the 1988 National Book Critics Circle Award for fiction. *Jasmine* was published in 1989. Mukherjee joined the University of California at Berkeley as distinguished professor in 1989. *The Holder of the World*, a novel, was published in 1993. Another novel, *Leave It to Me*, followed in 1997. Her sixth novel is *Desirable Daughters* (2002).

Bharati Mukherjee's fiction began to receive sustained attention from literary critics in the 1990s. Conference presentations on Mukherjee's fiction are abundant, and presenters are both male and female, their interest suggesting that Mukherjee's narratives draw readers of both genders.

Published scholarship on Mukherjee is currently steeped in contro-

4. The Immigrants' Search for Identity

versy. In *Bharati Mukherjee* (1996), Fakrul Alam documents much of the critical controversy surrounding Mukherjee's own elitism and actual distance from the majority of South Asian immigrants in North America. Alam cautiously concludes that "She has taken American fiction in new directions and can claim to be a major ethnic woman writer of contemporary America" (147). Alam commends Mukherjee, who

> has been able to give her firsthand experience of exile, expatriation, and immigration her considerable narrative skills and a lively imagination to produce memorable and colorful tales of the excitement as well as the traumas of adjusting to a new world [*Bharati Mukherjee* 147].

Most of the criticism that Fakrul Alam responds to appears in a collection of twelve critical essays edited by Emmanuel S. Nelson and titled *Bharati Mukherjee: Critical Perspectives* (1993). In the introduction to this volume, Nelson states that the purpose of the collection is to broaden "the parameters of the discussion that began at the 1991 MLA convention special session on Bharati Mukherjee" and to acknowledge "Mukherjee's emergence as a major American writer with an international audience" (xvii).

In this volume Maya Manju Sharma defends Mukherjee's early novels *Wife* and *The Tiger's Daughter* against the attacks of both Indian nationalists and white feminists. Sharma concludes that

> The easy rhetoric of colonialism and de-colonization does not have much to do with immigrant life in America...: Accepting the role of immigrant, she has not redefined herself as an American. Rather, she has consented to be part of that long procession of peoples who have over the years redefined America [20].

Although critics of South Asian origin frequently emphasize Mukherjee's Indian, Hindu, and Bengali philosophical biases, Mukherjee's themes and characters suggest that she is more than a "major ethnic woman writer" because her handling of the immigrant experience transcends ethnic borders. Mukherjee herself points out:

> I see a strong likeness between my writing and Bernard Malamud's, in spite of the fact that he describes the lives of the East European Jewish immigrants and I talk about newcomers from the Third World. Like Malamud, I write about a minority community which escapes the ghetto and adapts itself to the patterns of the dominant American culture. Like Malamud's, my work seems to find quite naturally a moral center [Carb 650].

Carole Stone points out close parallels between Malamud's and Mukherjee's fiction as each speaks about the diasporic experience of cultural alienation and addresses the renewing of oneself as an American. While Malamud keeps his male immigrant character within the Yiddish tradition of the *shlemiel,* a loser who earns our empathy through his humanity, Mukherjee breaks her readers' identification by portraying the female immigrant as a conquering heroine ("Malamud and Mukherjee" 214).

Stone also compares Malamud's humor to a sense of joy in Mukherjee's work. Stone emphasizes the fact that Mukherjee knew Malamud personally: "her husband Clark Blaise studied with Malamud at a Harvard Summer School Writing Workshop" (215). Stone suggests that by adopting Malamud as "a Western literary model" Mukherjee was moving away from the influence of V.S. Naipaul "to accelerate her assimilation into the American cultural center" (215). To adopt Victor Ramraj's terms, Mukherjee is an assimilationist who ridicules the traditionalist immigrant and explores the divided self of the first-generation assimilationist immigrant from South Asia.

Mukherjee's protagonists pursue their search for identity both as South Asians and as Americans in novels as different from one another as *Wife, Jasmine,* and *The Holder of the World.* Discussing Mukherjee's poetics, Fakrul Alam summarizes the changes in her narrative method:

> When she began writing, Mukherjee chose the omniscient point of view and habitually used irony in her work in a conscious bid to distance herself from her heroine. Now that she has dedicated herself to celebrating immigrant voices instead of treating the life of exiles and expatriates with condescension, Mukherjee has tried to minimize the distance between herself and her readers. This has meant that the ironic tone adopted in her earlier works has been replaced by a more intimate perspective [*Bharati Mukherjee* 13].

Mukherjee's first novel, *The Tiger's Daughter* (1972), narrates the experiences of Tara Banerjee Cartwright, who is visiting Calcutta. The novel received excellent reviews. Maya Manju Sharma states, "That Tara is the alter ego of the author is clear from the autobiographical details in *Days and Nights*; the testings of Tara are also battles in the growth of the author's sensibility from that of the expatriate to that of the immigrant"(5). Mukherjee brings to life the political and economic chaos of life in Calcutta in the late 1960s and early 1970s. Tara thinks of Calcutta as the deadliest city in the world. Tara's husband, who reads her reports as well as Ved Mehta's autobiographical narratives on India in *The New Yorker*, finds that

Calcutta was synonymous with garbage, disease and stagnation. Fakrul Alam points out that "Mukherjee has acknowledged in her interviews that she had set out in her first novel to deliberately mimic and subvert *A Passage to India*"(24).

The Tiger's Daughter was followed by the combined journals of Clark Blaise and Bharati Mukherjee, titled *Days and Nights in Calcutta* (1977). During the composition of *Days and Nights in Calcutta*, Mukherjee wrote her second novel, *Wife* (1975), which centers on the alienation and madness of an Indian immigrant housewife, named Dimple, in North America. *Wife* is the critique of traditional Indian society in which marriage was the only career choice open to young women. *Wife* predates the women's movement in India, which began in the 1980s. There is a streak of violence in Dimple Bose (nee Dasgupta) that is evident in her early days in Calcutta when she brings on a miscarriage by skipping rope in the early stages of a pregnancy. She also smashes a mouse and cockroaches, giving vent to her inner rage and violence. Among the early indications of her potential for killing is an episode where she buys a goldfish and flushes it down a toilet in an attempt to contain her violent urges on a limited scale.

Dimple arrives in New York in the second part of the novel as the wife of an Indian immigrant engineer from whom she is increasingly alienated. At first, she is entertained by the seemingly happy and prosperous company of Indian immigrants whom she meets. Then she finds herself confined to the Indian expatriate community and its traditional roles for women. She becomes depressed. Isolated from mainstream American society, confined to her apartment and the television set, Dimple is terrified by the violence of the world outside. Dimple slips deeper and deeper into a depression and the old thoughts of suicide from her Calcutta days return. Her husband, Amit Bose, is well-meaning but insensitive. He has his own share of problems adjusting to the immigrant life. According to Janet M. Powers,

> Amit, meanwhile, struggles to retain proper authority in the marriage, insisting that television, other Indians, and a baby are enough to keep any wife occupied.... He is, in fact, utterly irrational. Although he doesn't want Dimple to wear pants, he persuades her to drink beer. He memorizes jokes (five a day) methodically in an effort to become more like the Americans he works with. He urges Dimple to go out and meet other Indians but won't permit her to accept a job offered by one ["Sociopolitical Critique" 95].

At the center of Dimple's dilemma is the conflict between her need to find herself and the role of the "good Hindu wife," Sita of the *Ramayana*, which the Hindu Indian culture has imposed her on her. Dimple's conflict is inward as well as outward. On the outside, we see Dimple's eventual rejection of her two possible role models for immigrant women. One is Meena Sen, who clings to the Asian way of life so fiercely in New York that white Americans are not permitted inside her apartment. The other extreme is Ina Mullick, a bitterly unhappy Bengali wife who wears pants and a shirt that exposes her navel. She chain-smokes and is attending night school. Ina is ridiculed by the expatriate Indian community.

Dimple begins with the role model of Sita, but she eventually disintegrates into depression and madness. Janet M. Powers aptly comments that

> Like Sita, the good Hindu wife, Dimple has left Calcutta and gone with her husband to the "forest," enduring not only physical discomfort but also psychological distress. Yet because of the prison inadvertently created by Dimple's fear of New York City, her insensitive husband, and the expected immigrant wife's role, she becomes vulnerable to "kidnapping" by Milt Glasser, who is Ravana in American guise. Unlike Sita, Dimple does not insist on chastity; nor does she reward the husband who tries, belatedly, to rescue her from despondency. The flames in which she is tested are those of reality, but because she cannot truly be Sita, she does not survive, but implodes like a star ["Sociopolitical Critique" 94].

As her limited hold on reality gives way, and as she had frequently seen on television, Dimple sneaks up on Amit and stabs him to death from behind. The killing of Amit is an act neither of liberation nor of desperation, but one that symbolizes the inner and outer chaos of Dimple's own self. Dimple never fully comprehends the violence within herself even as she develops an unhealthy interest in the violence reported on American television.

The anarchy of the self experienced by Dimple in Mukherjee's *Wife* becomes a recurring motif in the numerous satirical portraits of South Asian immigrants in her collections of short fiction—*Darkness* (1983), and *Middleman and Other Stories* (1988). The influence of Bernard Malamud is clearly noticeable in *Darkness*. Naipaul and Malamud had become Mukherjee's literary models at this phase of her career. Fakrul Alam aptly comments that "If Malamud's humanism has inspired some of Mukherjee's tales of immigrant lives, others employ the kind of irony she had learned from Naipaul in presenting people who cannot or will not graft themselves into another culture"(51).

The comparison with Jewish American fiction is also pursued by Carole Stone, who writes that

> For while Jews have by the eighties become a familiar presence in

the American immigrant experience, the new Asian immigrants are viewed with suspicion. Mukherjee's fiction provides these new Americans with a voice which contributes to the discourse of marginality. Like the characters of her stories, Mukherjee, too, is a new arrival, pushing from the margins.... Mukherjee's fiction energizes moral concerns with its attention to Asian customs, religious, social structures, and political upheavals ["Malamud and Mukherjee" 224].

Bharati Mukherjee felt that she saw aspects of her own expatriate South Asian self in her own characters. In her introduction to *Darkness*, Bharati Mukherjee explained her point of view. She wrote:

> I have joined imaginative forces with an anonymous, driven, underclass of semi-assimilated Indians with sentimental attachments to a distant homeland but no real desire for permanent return. I see my "immigrant story" replicated in a dozen American cities, and instead of seeing my Indianness as a fragile identity to be preserved against obliteration (or worse, a "visible" disfigurement to be hidden), I see it now as a set of fluid identities to be celebrated. I see myself as an American writer in the tradition of other American writers whose parents or grandparents had passed through Ellis Island. Indianness is now a metaphor, a particular way of comprehending the world [*Darkness* 3].

To adopt Victor Ramraj's terminology, Mukherjee views herself as an *arriver*, celebrating South Asian immigrants who live in a perpetual enigma of *arrival* on the North American continent.

The cultural confusion of Mukherjee's characters is presented with comic realism. In an earlier essay, one of the present authors comments that

> In Mukherjee's short fiction, the satiric narrative contrasts interior monologues with public actions as the principal device by which characters confront their own concealed desires. By this process, Mukherjee's protagonists discover the new, at times fragile identities that they have fashioned in the new country [Pati 198].

A typical instance of such an interior monologue occurs in "The Lady from Lucknow," in which the female protagonist reflects on her affair with James Beamish:

> I had thought myself provocative and fascinating. What had begun as an adventure had become shabby and complex. I was just

another involvement of a white man in a pokey little outpost, something that "men do" and then come to their senses while the *memsahibs* drink gin and tonic and fan their faces. I didn't merit a stab wound through the heart [*Darkness* 33].

The South Asian speaker perceives her own arrival, her lack of assimilation, her own marginalized condition. This character's predicament may be summed up in C. L. Chua's observation that "Several fictions of V. S. Naipaul and Bharati Mukherjee have dealt poignantly with the experience of Indians making the passage from India, depicting the dreamers with realism and questioning the dream with irony" ("Passages from India" 51).

Similarly, the traditionalist Mr. Bhowmick in "A Father" is an example of an Indian dreamer who cannot return to the city he left (*Darkness* 65). Mr. Bhowmick remains an arriver. However, his dream does not include his Americanized daughter:

Babli was not the child he would have chosen as his only heir. She was brighter certainly than the sons and daughters of the other Bengalis he knew in Detroit, and she had been the only female student in most of her classes at Georgia Tech, but as she sat there in her beige linen business suit, her thick chin dropping into a polka-dotted cravat, he regretted again that she was not the child of his dreams.... She wasn't womanly or tender the way that unmarried girls had been in the wistful days of his adolescence [*Darkness* 63].

Mr. Bhowmick's powerlessness in an alien culture and in his home is emphasized in "A Father."

Bhowmick worships Kali, the goddess of wrath and vengeance. Silently, he watches Babli's pregnancy progress, ready to assimilate a white son-in-law if necessary.... Babli's sarcastic comparison of her artificially inseminated pregnancy to the practice of marriages of convenience in India brings her father's violence upon her amid her mother's hysteria. Finally, Mrs. Bhowmick calls the police [Pati 203].

In *Middleman and Other Stories* (1988), Mukherjee explores the experiences of immigrant Asian women more closely. In "A Wife's Story," the central character Panna, who is clearly an *arriver*, soliloquizes:

I've made it. I'm making something of my life. I've left home, my husband, to get a Ph.D. in Special Ed. I have a multiple-entry visa and a small scholarship for two years. After that, we'll see. My mother was beaten by her mother-in-law, my grandmother, when she'd registered for French lessons at the Alliance Francaise. My grandmother, the eldest daughter of a rich zamindar, was illiterate [*Middleman* 29].

The most powerful interior monologue in *The Middleman* is that of Shaila Bhave, a thirty-six-year-old Indian-born Canadian whose husband and two sons die in the terrorist bombing of an Air India plane. In "The Management of Grief," Shaila concludes:

> Then as I stood in the path looking north to Queen's park and west to the university, I heard the voices of my family one last time. *Your time has come,* they said, *Go, be brave.*
> I do not know where this voyage I have begun will end. I do not know which direction I will take. I dropped the package on a park bench and started walking [*Middleman* 197].

Shaila Bhave's tragedy changes her from an arriver to a permanent inhabitant of the New World, albeit a confused one.

Even though Bhave's grief leaves her without any sense of direction in an alien and materialistic culture, in *Jasmine* (1989), the central character battles adversity by transforming herself repeatedly to cope with the challenges of being in the New World. The novel contains the powerful message that the assimilationist must undergo inner and outer transformation in order to survive the ordeal of arrival both physically and emotionally.

There is a story titled "Jasmine" in *The Middleman* about a girl from Trinidad who enters America illegally. The novel of the same name, however, is the story of the adventures of a young Indian widow. Gurleen Grewal takes a negative view of *Jasmine* in her essay "Born Again American: The Immigrant Consciousness in *Jasmine*." However, she concedes that the novel "is an immigrant *Bildungsroman* because it posits a norm of self-development" (182).

The six stages in Jasmine's development and transformation are symbolized in the different names that others give her. Her parents name her Jyoti; her husband, Lillian Gordon, calls her Jazzy; Taylor uses Jase; and Bud's name for her is Jane.

The transformations and reincarnations of Jasmine, the young Hindu widow from Punjab who becomes Jane Ripplemeyer, the twenty-four-year-old common-law wife of a Midwestern banker, do not bring about a "willing suspension of disbelief" in many of Mukherjee's critics. Flaws in the plotting and characterization of *Jasmine* have been pointed out by most critics of the novel. *Jasmine* is also disappointing as a portrait of a liberated woman because Jasmine is largely dependent on men at the different stages of her transformations. From a superstitious Hindu widow she becomes an American gold digger.

Marginalized as a poor widow in the Old World, she continues to be marginalized as an illegal immigrant temptress figure in America. C. L. Chua is an apologist for her reincarnations when he writes,

> Mukherjee's Jasmine, therefore, emerges as a woman who has decidedly overcome her gender handicap.... Unlike Naipaul's Santosh, who is only *free from*, Mukherjee's Jasmine is *free to*. Though not without pain and ambiguity, Jasmine's experience forms, on the whole, a positive and optimistic pattern for South Asians in the New World; for Jasmine has indeed come a long way, not only from the Punjab to California, but also from believing that a wife's virtue entails self-immolation to believing that a pregnant woman's happiness justifies her deserting the crippled father of her unborn child for the arms of a lover ["Passages from India" 59].

Early in the novel, the protagonist discovers that her new life in an alien culture is without morality when she kills her rapist: "What a monstrous thing, an infinitesimal thing, is the taking of a human life; for the second time in three months, I was in a room with a *slain* man, my body bloodied. I was walking death. Death incarnate" (*Jasmine* 119).

Jasmine's new world of the illegal immigrant is a perpetual war zone where she seems to live in the way of the early Americans on the frontier: "I buttoned up the jacket and sat by the fire. With the first streaks of dawn, my first full American day, I walked out the front drive of the motel to the highway and began my journey, traveling light" (*Jasmine* 121). Jasmine's philosophy is a satiric concoction of the Hindu beliefs in reincarnation and the lawless practices of survival on the American frontier:

> Adventure, risk, transformation: the frontier is pushing indoors through uncaulked windows. Watch me re-position the stars, I whisper to the astrologer who floats cross-legged above my kitchen stove [*Jasmine* 240].

In her constant memories of death, Jasmine discovers her true affinity with Du, the orphaned teenage refugee, her stepson:

> The smell of singed flesh is always with me. Du and I have seen death up close. We've stowed away on boats like Half-Face's, we've hurtled through time tunnels. We've seen the worst and survived. Like creatures in fairy tales, we've shrunk and we've swollen and we've swallowed the cosmos whole [*Jasmine* 240].

4. The Immigrants' Search for Identity

Jasmine's transformations do not bring the happiness and love she seeks. Chua reminds readers that Mukherjee offers a more positive portrayal of immigrant life in America than V.S. Naipaul, although the American Dream can easily become a nightmare for immigrants (60). Such attempts in the literary history of the novel go back as far as the British novelist Defoe's *Moll Flanders*. Jasmine is a South Asian Moll Flanders who has some parallels with Hannah Easton, the Salem Bibi of Mukherjee's *The Holder of the World* (1993).

Jasmine is ultimately a daring attempt at picaresque novel. If *Jasmine* fails to bring about a complete suspension of disbelief because of Mukherjee's intertwining of reality and myth in a contemporary American setting, the change of setting to the seventeenth century in *The Holder of the World* (1993) works somewhat better for Mukherjee's art of mythmaking.

Fakrul Alam finds that in *The Holder of the World* Mukherjee has become more of a mainstream American writer (*Bharati Mukherjee* 119). Alam concludes that "The theme of the subtle relatedness of lives is, of course, a development of the theme of immigration that Mukherjee celebrated in the third phase of her career in that she is going beyond the recent wave of immigration from Asia to America to exult in the movement across oceans and frontiers across the centuries" (124).

The first-person narrator of *The Holder of the World*, Beigh Masters, lives with her lover, Venn Iyer, a second-generation Asian Indian whose research is directed at "constructing an interactive model of historical or imaginative reality" (*The Holder of the World* 35). Beigh herself is intensely involved with historical research. Like Mukherjee's other female protagonists, she expresses herself in frequent interior monologues.

> I drove out to this museum to track down for a client what he claims is the most perfect diamond in the world. The diamond has a name: the Emperor's Tear. For eleven years, I have been tracking the Salem Bibi, a woman from Salem who ended up in the Emperor's court. I know her as well as any scholar has known her subject; I know her like a doctor and lawyer, like a mother and daughter. With every new thing I've learned, I've come imperceptibly closer to the Emperor's Tear. In that final Gotterdammerung painting, she is holding it: I have seen the Emperor's Tear atop its golden orb. Three hundred years ago, it existed in her hands; I know where she came from and where she went. I couldn't care less about the Emperor's Tear, by now. I only care about Salem Bibi [*The Holder of the World* 19].

Beigh Masters discerns a similarity between herself and the women characters she has researched. She finds a striking parallel in women's interest in and love for men of "other" cultures, a fascination symbolic of excitement and adventure:

> Like Rebecca, I have a lover. One who would seem alien to my family. A lover scornful of our habits of self-effacement and reasonableness, of our naive or desperate clinging to an imagined community. Venn was born in India and came over as a baby. His family are all successful, there was never question of anything different. He grew up in a world so secure I can't imagine it, where for us security is another kind of trap, something to be discarded as dramatically as Rebecca stepped out of dog-blooded widow's weeds into a life of sin and servitude [*Holder* 31].

Most of Beigh's narrative is about the life and adventures of Salem Bibi, or Hannah Easton Fitch Legge, the adopted daughter of a New England Puritan family, who marries the dashing sea captain Gabriel Legge in 1692 and leaves America. Gabriel leaves her in England when he is on the sea. Then he joins the East India Company and moves her to the southeastern coast (Coromandel) of India. Gabriel takes an uneducated Indian mistress and turns pirate. Left on her own, Hannah has her own adventures in India. In a sense, Hannah's whole life and imagination have been focused on exotic adventures. As a child, she was an artist with her embroidery. Beigh describes Hannah's work:

> On a field of light blue, Hannah created an "uttermost shore." A twelve-year-old Puritan orphan who had never been out of Massachusetts imagined an ocean, palm trees, thatched cottages, and black-skinned men casting nets and colorfully garbed bare-breasted women mending them; native barks and, on the horizon, high-masted schooners. Colonial gentlemen in breeches and ruffled lace, buckled hats and long black coats pacing the shore. In the distance, through bright green foliage, a ghostly white building—it could even be the Taj Mahal—is rising [*Holder* 44].

Fakrul Alam interprets Hannah's affair with the Hindu king, Rajah Jadav Singh, as an episode of sexual awakening and sexual fulfillment. However, the reader is prepared for Hannah's tropical romance much earlier. Her embroidery itself displays the impassioned and adventurous nature that is restrained in a Puritan community:

> Her embroidery gave away the conflict she tried so hard to deny or suppress. She knew she must deny all she'd seen the night of her mother's disappearance and all she felt, for she, worthless sin-

ner and daughter of Satan's lover, had been taken in and raised by decent souls [*Holder* 42].

Hannah finally returns to New England and raises her daughter, Pearl, Rajah Jadav Singh's child. She locates her mother, Rebecca Easton, and they live together on the margin of a Puritan community. Not only in the naming of Pearl, but also in its allusion to John Hawthorne, the ancestor of Nathaniel Hawthorne, Mukherjee's novel attempts to anchor itself in the mainstream of American fiction.

Alam finds that *The Holder of the World* can claim metafictional status because it contains enough comments within it to make us aware of its status as a "fictional artifact" (Bharati Mukherjee 133). He compares Beigh to the writer Mukherjee (130–131). *The Holder*, like *Jasmine*, contains occasionally unconvincing metamorphoses of characters. Unlike *Jasmine*, the later novel's sudden transformations are limited to Hannah's Indian maid Bhagmati. Overall, *The Holder of the World* is much more convincing in its use of multiple voices, plot construction, and characterization because its historical setting lends itself more readily to adventure and romance than does the contemporary setting of *Jasmine*.

In the reader's guide, published as an unpaginated appendix with *Leave It to Me*, is an interview in which Mukherjee claims that

> Actually, I think of my last three novels, *Jasmine*, *The Holder of the World*, and *Leave It to Me*, as a trilogy. The protagonist of each novel—Jyoti/Jasmine, Hannah/Salem Bibi, and Debby/Devi—is a strong woman who longs for a world that's more just and generous than the one she inherited at birth. These women are also bold enough to act out their dreams. They are idealists and romantics; and because of this, they are also restless. But each woman responds in her unique way to dreams for a better life.... Debby is a multiracial orphan, born and abandoned in India, then adopted by an American family in upstate New York. She is confused, hurt, and angry. She has to sort through her various racial, cultural, social heritages before she can be at peace with herself. I think of Debby as the difficult sister of Jasmine. These three characters are very real to me. They are still carrying on their lives inside my head [*Leave It to Me* n. p.].

This novel combines fantasy and reality with a clear attempt to return to the picaresque mode of *Jasmine*. However, in *Leave It To Me* the protagonist's quest is to learn the identity of her biological parents. The plot connects Devi's early life in India with her adult life in America to create a parody of the 1960s counterculture, as Fred Pointer, who is searching for Devi's parents, states:

> "I've exchanged a couple of faxes with a fellow in Bombay. I worked on a case with this fellow must have been five years ago. He didn't recognize the name you gave, but he said he remembered there'd been juicy stuff in all the papers about a sex-guru serial killer and his harem of white hippies, he thought way back in the seventies. He's checking it out" [*Leave It to Me* 105].

The second half of the novel is set in Berkeley, and the contemporary lives of former hippies are depicted in a recognizable tone of satire. Devi finds out that her middle-aged boyfriend Ham was also her biological mother's lover in his youth:

> Better that I had been the fetus Jess aborted. "Ham," I murmured, "why didn't you ask Jess to marry you?"
> "The times, love. Marriage and commitment were for the bourgeois." He tucked his shirt back into his pants.
> "You should have married her." I kicked Ham's shoes and socks across the floor [*Leave It to Me* 231].

The Electra myth that weaves together the different strands of the plot, as Devi finds the identity of her biological parents, culminates in Devi killing her biological father, who has just beheaded Ham at the horrifying conclusion of the novel:

> *Violent propensities.* The sea has them, the Earth rocks with them. I claim my inheritance, kneeing Bio-Dad so hard as he tilts his head back to draw from the tiny bottle that it tumbles him. TAPE ROLLING. The cleaver fuses to my arm. It soars and plunges, soars and plunges. "Monster!" I scream. I keep screaming as I cradle Ham's tormented face to my bosom. I am screaming as I dial 911 [*Leave It to Me* 235].

Even as Devi/Debby discovers her "violent propensities" and possibly dies or disappears when the houseboat goes up in flames, we are reminded that philosophically, none of Mukherjee's protagonists achieve significant feats of self-realization or self-actualization. Such a conclusion suggests Mukherjee's own skepticism about the immigrant experience in which the quest or journey itself is symbolic of inner wanderings and indecisions. The diasporic experience is that of a divided self and a fractured world for immigrants both traditionalist and assimilationist.

Bharati Mukherjee's *Desirable Daughters* (2002) continues in her earlier mode of narrative, that of the immigrant's tale. The plot develops around three sisters of a Calcutta-based Bengali Brahmin family whose fictional upbringing is very much like the author's own background. These are the three "desirable daughters" of the novel's title. The author possibly uses autobiographical experiences of her own youth as well as field observations based upon her current California residency. Like *Jasmine* and *Leave It to Me*, this novel has a plot with murder, crime, violence, and mysterious criminal strangers.

The novel is narrated from the point of view of Tara, the youngest sister. Tara is the divorced spouse of an Indian-born industrial tycoon in California. She works in a primary school as a volunteer. Tara lives with her teenage son Rabi, who comes out of the closet by revealing his homosexual preferences. Tara is stalked by a man who claims to be the illegitimate son of her New Jersey–resident sister, Padma Mehta. He claims that he was given up for adoption because of the hypocrisy and bigotry of the Old World. The unfolding plot reveals that he is not Padma's son but an impostor who has murdered the son and assumed his identity.

The police officer assigned to Tara's case is an Indian American member of the San Francisco Police Department. The San Francisco PD is also investigating other criminal rings from the Indian subcontinent within its jurisdiction. Mukherjee paints a sinister picture of ethnic America with all sorts of bizarre characters and their contradictions. When Tara arrives at her sister's home on the east coast, she is pushed towards re-entry into a traditionalist immigrant community. Mukherjee's descriptions create a picture of Jackson Heights, with its Little India, that is almost documentary in the quality of its descriptive details. During Tara's east coast visit, the idea of sacred sisterhood is totally debunked by the author. Towards the end, events take an unexpected turn as Tara's ex-husband Bish comes to Tara's house only to become the victim of a bomb attack, presumably by the stalker.

In the background of Tara's contemporary experience is the story of Tara's ancestor, the Tree Bride, an Indian freedom fighter of the nineteenth century. False fronts and hypocrisy abound as Mukherjee continues to satirize the second-generation South Asians who have "made it" to success in America. In terms of narrative genre this novel is an interesting composite of immigrant narrative, satire, and suspense. The episodes are loosely connected, somewhat like Divakaruni's recent fiction.

Overall, Mukherjee's most recent novel has dramatic energy comparable with Anitav Ghosh's *The Calcutta Chromosome*, although there are some disappointing sections where Mukherjee resorts to the use of stereotypes, perhaps with little factual basis.

Like Bharati Mukherjee, Chitra Banerjee Divakaruni came to the United States for higher education. Divakaruni lived in India until 1976. Coming to the U.S. at the age of nineteen, she has held many odd jobs in the service industry. She earned an M.A. in English from Wright State University, Ohio, and a Ph.D. from the University of California at Berkeley. Currently a professor of creative writing at the University of Houston, Divakaruni has been the president of MAITRI, a helpline for South Asian women victims of domestic abuse, since 1991.

Divakaruni began as a poet, then turned her hand to fiction. Her first short-story collection, *Arranged Marriage* (1995), was an instant success. Working with partially autobiographical materials, Divakaruni depicts men and women seeking to break down the barriers between the Old World of their origin and the New World of their adoption. Many narratives use a woman's point of view. Her work is frequently discussed by women scholars, suggesting that she targets a largely female reading public and gender issues among South Asians.

Divakaruni's *Arranged Marriage* and Mukherjee's *Jasmine* are both accused by fiction writer Samrat Upadhyay of "exoticizing their country to cater to the fast palates of Americans" (3). Upadhyay complains of a biased depiction of gender roles in the fiction of Divakaruni and Mukherjee:

> This selective representation also happens in Divakaruni's portrayal of Indian women, who find themselves suffocating under the burden and constraints of traditional arranged marriage, whose husbands are invariably insensitive, controlling louts (even the educated ones).... This emphasis on discarding one's roots and assimilating into the mainstream American society has been the backbone of Bharati Mukherjee's fiction, and now we see the same equation (Western values = Emancipation) in Divakaruni's work ["Between Third World and First" 3].

Upadhyay touches upon a vital issue, the American heritage of Mukherjee's and Divakaruni's fiction. The demonizing of the Asian male for his insensitivity in his relationships with women in comparison to the white American male or the Asian American male (Westernized Asian male) is also observed in the fiction of Asian American writer Amy Tan. This motif in South Asian fiction can be traced to earlier depictions of Asian males and Asian females in the American media. Commenting on racism in the visual media, Eugene F. Wong points out that "both sexism and racism have been blended together to produce the sexualization of white racism—with its emphasis upon the negativity of Asian males and positivity of Asian females" (*On Visual Media Racism* 260).

Divakaruni's women characters, like Mukherjee's, frequently find themselves in a confusing multicultural New World society in the company of male characters who are either losers or antiheroes. Out of these

4. The Immigrants' Search for Identity

failed relationships emerges a search for identity. For instance, in the poignant story "Clothes," the first-person narrator arrives in America to discover that her husband is struggling to make a living out of a Seven-Eleven store, supporting his parents and newlywed wife. The narrator dreams of making money for herself and her husband Somesh:

> Meanwhile I will the store to make money for us. Quickly. Because when we move, we'll be paying for two households. But so far it hasn't worked. They're running at a loss, Somesh tells me. They had to let the hired help go. This means some nights Somesh has to take the graveyard shift (that horrible word, like a cold hand up my spine) because his partner refuses to go [*Arranged Marriage* 27].

Her dreams are short-lived, as Somesh is shot and killed one night in a robbery at his store. Like Jasmine in Mukherjee's novel, the narrator realizes that America is a land of violence as her girlish dreams are shattered forever.

Similarly in "Silver Pavements," a youthful Indian woman arrives at the home of her "rich" American relatives to discover that her uncle is a struggling auto mechanic who has not achieved the American dream. Her aunt lives housebound in a tough neighborhood. The uncle warns the narrator of the problems of anti-Asian racism:

> Now my Uncle's tone is dark and raw. The bitterness in it coats my mouth like the karela juice my Mother used to give me to cool my liver.
>
> "The Americans hate us. They're always putting us down because we're dark-skinned foreigners, *kala admi*. Blaming us for the damned economy, for taking away their jobs. You'll see it for yourself soon enough" [*Arranged Marriage* 43].

Venturing out with her aunt into the streets, the narrator undergoes an unpleasant initiation into the racism of the New World as their coats are soiled by white boys throwing slush at them and calling them "nigger" (*Arranged Marriage* 51). The aunt's pacifism is born of knowledge— minorities cannot fight back with ease or sureness of victory. The narrator realizes what it means to be a minority in an alien culture.

Along with the issues of racism and violence raised by Divakaruni's fiction, there are recurring depictions of marriages that are far from ideal. Divakaruni places the responsibility for flawed marriages mainly on the lack of self-awareness in the protagonists. For instance, in the "The Disappearance," the husband who is left with the son remains in denial of the underlying problems that existed in his marriage prior to his wife's disappearance:

> Later he would think about what the policeman had asked, while he sat in front of the computer in his office, or while he lay in the bed which still seemed to smell of her. (But surely that was his imagination—the linen had been washed already.) He had told the truth about them not having a quarrel, hadn't he? ...
> They hadn't really had a fight. She wasn't, thank God, the quarrelsome type.... Hush now, she would tell the boy, settle down and they would walk over sedately to give him his welcome-home kiss [*Arranged Marriage* 170–171].

Even as he reflects on his marriage, the narrator disregards what he knows to be a fact—that he raped his wife over and over again.

Just as the narrator of "The Disappearance" denies the reality of his abuse of his wife, the narrator of "A Perfect Life" reminisces about her one attempt at motherhood—sheltering a seven-year-old runaway boy, Krishna. While she has never wanted to become like her girlfriends whose lives are ruled by the tyranny of red-faced babies and small children, she realizes that in choosing the "entirely civilized" European American boyfriend, Richard, she must bid farewell to her motherly inclinations forever:

> Richard and I are back together again, and last month when I finally wrote my mother about him, she surprised me by being far less upset than I'd feared. Maybe she figured that even a foreign husband—a *firingi*—is better than no husband at all. At any rate, she's planning to attend our wedding, which is to be this June, followed by a honeymoon in the South of France. I haven't yet told her I agreed to the marriage only on the condition that we don't have any children [*Arranged Marriage* 107].

The title, "A Perfect Life," satirizes the emptiness of the narrator's life with its fine job and perfect husband.

Divakaruni's first novel, *The Mistress of Spices* (1997), utilizes the genre of the fairy tale. The appeal of this genre for Divakaruni is also evident in her second novel, *Sister of My Heart* (1999), in which the two main characters invent their own fairy tales to come to terms with decisive moments in their lives. The first-person narrator of *The Mistress of Spices* is Tilottama (Tilo), an enchantress from another century who has been trained in charms and spells using common Indian spices. This immortal mistress has been sent by supernatural forces, in the assumed body of an elderly

Indian woman, to run a small South Asian spice store in Oakland, California. Possessing the supernatural power of reading people's innermost thoughts and desires, Tilo becomes a savior of troubled South Asian immigrants such as Ahuja's battered wife, the schoolboy Jaggi, Haroun the taxi driver, and the traditionalist family of the young woman Geeta, who is in love with her Mexican American supervisor at work.

Assisting confused South Asian immigrants in resolving their differences within and without, Tilo becomes aware of her own difference—her immortal life, her magical powers, and the vow of celibacy she took centuries ago when the First Mother invoked the Hindu mythological connotation of her name: "When Brahma made Tilottama to be chief dancer in Indra's court, he warned her never to give her love to man—only to the dance" (*Mistress* 45). Predictably, Tilo falls in love with a man named Raven, who is himself marginal in American society in that he is half white and half Native American. After a while, she discovers that he reciprocates her friendship, each one viewing the other as foreign and romantic: "Each of us loving not the other but the exotic image of the other that we have fashioned out of our own lack" (*Mistress* 331).

The romance is described in poetic terms as Tilo uses her spices and spells to transform herself into a beautiful young woman. After the first date, Tilo expects to die for having broken her vow. Instead, there is an earthquake which destroys her spice shop. She is rescued from the debris by Raven, and she chooses mortal life with him over living as an immortal mistress of spices. The American male–Asian female romance is an expected conclusion. There is a tongue-in-cheek quality to the novel's closure whereby Tilo chooses assimilation into American society as a South Asian immigrant over immortality!

In *Mistress of Spices*, Divakaruni develops the stylistic technique of using words in Indian languages—the Indian names of spices, for example—for ambiance:

> And so I call on ginger.
> Root of gnarled wisdom, *ada* in your hide of banded brown, help me in this my seeking. I weigh your speckled solidness in the hollow of my palm. Wash you three times in lime water. Slice you translucent-thin as the curtains between waking and dream.
> *Adrak* ginger, be with me.
> I drop the slices in a pan of boiling water, watch them rise and sink, rise and sink, in a slow whirl. Like lives caught on karma's wheel. Steam fills my kitchen, clings haze-heavy to my lashes so it is hard to see. Steam and that wild smell like bamboo grass torn and chewed that will stay in my sari long after [*Mistress of Spices* 133].

The selective use of Indian loan words also reinforces Tilo's South Asian voice. The same stylistic feature appears in Divakaruni's second novel, *Sister of My Heart*, where the words in Bengali and the fairy tales and fables of the old aunt and the main characters almost create a poetic sub-text.

Sister of My Heart (1999) juxtaposes the two first-person narratives of the Chatterjee cousins Anju and Sudha, who grow up in Calcutta in a community of women—mothers, aunt, maid. The inseparable cousins are born on the same day, and both of their fathers are believed to have died on a trip to the forest to find a cave of rubies. The only man they see every day is their chauffeur Singhji, who is disfigured from facial burns. The novel is a South Asian *bildungsroman* which chronicles the childhood, adolescence, and adulthood of two females in a very conservative upper-middle-class home in Calcutta in the 1980s. Sudha, the beautiful daughter of the family's black sheep, rejects a young admirer to marry the husband chosen by her mother. Even though Sudha's husband is kind at first, life in the extended family under a cruel and controlling mother-in-law is an extended nightmare that culminates in divorce papers being sent to Sudha when she refuses to abort the baby girl she is expecting. Meanwhile, Anju, the daughter of the wealthy branch of the family, has married an Indian computer scientist working in America, who supports her college education. The cousins are reunited by Anju's efforts: Sudha and her baby Dayita come to visit Anju after Anju has a miscarriage brought on by working long hours to pay for Sudha's air ticket to America.

The narrators are disillusioned in their relationships with men who are essentially weak. The male characters are all demonized to some extent, even Sudha's long-lost adventurer father, who turns out to be Singhji. By choosing to remain in disguise as a chauffeur, he gets away from his nagging wife and family responsibilities while he can watch over his growing daughter. Even Sudha's long-suffering admirer Ashok is a flawed male in that he cannot at first accept Sudha's baby, whom she loves. Although Ashok comes around, Sudha realizes that her greatest emotional bond is with her cousin; and that economic self-reliance, as well as realizing her dream of designing clothes, is her basic goal just as Anju's is to complete her college education. While Anju and Sudha begin to seek ways of fulfilling their dreams of self-reliance in America, the novel chronicles social reality in contemporary urban India, where easier divorce laws have undermined the stability of marriage as an institution of economic support for women. The use of amniocentesis to identify female fetuses that are then aborted is also a social evil whereby liberal abortion laws are used by unprincipled individuals.

Even as Sudha lands in America with her baby, Anju is still grieving for the loss of her baby in a miscarriage:

> No, I try to tell her. It would be disloyal to the dead. But she's already thrust the bundle into my arms. I'm surprised by how heavy it is for such a small creature. Its solid heft belies its frail appearance. How natural the head feels nestled in the curve of my shoulder. I'd promised myself I'd never hold another baby with the arms that belonged to Prem, but this—this is so *right*. As right as the ruby—yes, I recognized it at once—around her throat. Even the way she butts her face against my breast—she's hungry now—is more sweet than bitter. Inside me, love lets itself down in a rush, uncontrollable, like the milk when your baby cries [*Sister of My Heart* 321].

The close of the novel is ominous, for Anju has a premonition of hard times to come, a subject that is developed in *The Vine of Desire*:

> Somewhere Sunil drums his fingers on the edge of the baggage cart and says we really should be going, but we don't listen, not right away. There'll be trouble enough later—like an animal I sense it prickling the nape of my neck. I'll deal with it when it comes [*Sister of My Heart* 322].

A different set of human problems are depicted in the stories (several published previously) of *The Unknown Errors of Our Lives* (2001). Reviewer Mahadev Desai correctly observes the growth of Divakaruni's fictional techniques when he states,

> The nine riveting stories display rich imagery, piercing emotional truths, and psychological insights. The stories deal with the choices men, women, and children make at every stage of their lives and how the consequences of those decisions affect not only the decision makers, but also those they have left behind and those who are living with them in America. People change, places change, and relationships get twisted. In each story, there is an effort at realignment and a yearning to rekindle lost moments—if only in memory. Each story's journey has surprising twists and turns and ends in self-discovery ["Stories of Second Chances" 38].

The psychological realism and intensity of character development in some of the short stories in Divakaruni's latest anthology may be compared to the depth of characterization in Jhumpa Lahiri's Pulitzer Prize–winning anthology *The Interpreter of Maladies*. Many of the protagonists are sensitive and reflective women characters who try to comprehend and resolve the multitude of differences and contradictions they must often contend with to continue with their lives and to preserve their sanity. In the title story, Ruchira, a second-generation Indian American, comes to know that her fiancé's previous girlfriend is expecting his baby. She also learns that he gave the ex-girlfriend money for an abortion. In the midst of wedding preparations, Ruchira is disillusioned but she realizes that it may be better not to tell Biren: "Marriage is a long, hobbled race, learning the other's gait as you go, and thanks to Arlene she has a head start" ("Unknown Errors" 234). A similar startling realization comes to the protagonist of "The Blooming Season for Cacti," who learns that the Indian woman who is her landlady and roommate harbors a lesbian's love for her: "Who is to say? If a woman finds joy in the spare, pared flesh of the desert, if she finds joy in another woman's sand-brown body, who is to say?" (208).

The most powerful story of the collection, titled "Mrs. Dutta Writes a Letter," was previously anthologized in *Best American Short Stories 1999*. The story develops the tensions that arise in a South Asian home in California where the husband's mother has been invited to move in permanently. She comes after selling her home in Calcutta, and persists in her Old World ways of cooking and housework that bring conflict with her grandchildren and daughter-in-law. Her son Sagar is caught between mother and wife as the mother feels betrayed.

The cross-generational household conflict is not only a result of geographical differences; the problems are also universal, as housekeeping differences between mothers-in-law and daughters-in-law are well-known. Also, in many instances, the ultimate separation for an elderly person is the giving up of a home and the familiar habits of a lifetime to move into a relative's home or an assisted-living arrangement. While Mrs. Dutta realizes that she needs to adjust to America and her son's home, her pain is obvious: "When she opens them, nail marks line the soft flesh of her palms, red hieroglyphs—her body's language, telling her what to do" ("Mrs. Dutta Writes a Letter" 33).

Chitra Divakaruni's most recent novel, *The Vine of Desire* (2002), lacks the energy of her previous fiction. The winding threads of narrative in *Sister of My Heart* are followed up by a sequel in *The Vine of Desire*. This novel is another coming-to-America fictional work that deals with the arrival of Sudha and her daughter as house guests of Anju and her husband Sunil. Structurally, this novel combines third-person narratives, interior monologues of characters, letters, and even Anju's term papers. The collage-like narrative form is probably intended for verisimilitude, and the overall effect is to suggest that each one of the characters lives an isolated and even alienated existence. Living in a small California apartment, Sudha, Anju, and Sunil inhabit their own little separate worlds. These characters have totally separate histories, anxieties, hopes, and dreams.

All is not well in this New World immigrant narrative. The new setting creates major rifts in relationships. Anju's husband Sunil loves Sudha's baby daughter, Dayita. He is able to play a fatherly role in interacting with the baby. He also falls in love with Sudha and has sex with her, an act that leads to Sudha's moving out of the apartment altogether. While Anju pursues university education, writing, and self-discovery, Sunil asks her for a divorce. Never quite compatible, this couple's lives have gone different ways.

Sudha is pursued by Lalit, a second-generation Indian American. Lalit is a physician who is paying back heavy student loans. In this de-glamorization of the American experience from a new arriver's point of view, Sudha realizes that Lalit is attracted to her because he has an idealized and romantic vision of the "Indian woman," or the "nice" woman from an Old World culture.

Faced with Sunil and Lalit in America, and her boyfriend in India who is planning to come and take her home, Sudha leaves Anju's home with her daughter Dayita. She gets a job as the paid nurse for an elderly Indian man who has suffered a stroke. Like Sudha, her patient wants to return home. She reaches an understanding with him that she will return to India with him and work as his caregiver.

Pursued by three men for her good looks, Divakaruni's Sudha seeks independence and self-reliance. In this way, Sudha seeks to work free of "the vine of desire," and establishes an independent and self-reliant existence in economic terms. Sudha and her patient represent examples of the immigrants who return to the Old World having "failed" to achieve the American dream.

The novel stops rather than ends. Anju has taken up the new hobby of hang gliding, which is also a metaphor for the immigrant's dream that she and Sudha brought to America:

> Her first outing in America, the picnic on the beach, the Pacific blue as a flame, opening out and out the way she thought her life was going to. The hang gliders swooping down to flirt with the waves. The man who is not with them today [*The Vine of Desire* 368].

The novel's sudden closure suggests that there may be yet another sequel to *Sister of My Heart*. The novel also moves away from romantic love and confronts the economic aspect of heterosexual relationships in which the woman does not have an independent source of income. Sudha's flight from the three men and her quest for financial independence returns the reader to the fundamental feminist concept of "a room of one's own" put forth by Virginia Woolf at the beginning of the twentieth century ("A Room of One's Own" 2433).

Throughout the course of their fictional narratives, Mukherjee and Divakaruni suggest that South Asian women's lives have been permanently altered, not always for the better, in their New World immigrant experience.

5

New Voices: Bapsi Sidhwa, Jhumpa Lahiri, and Other Emerging Fiction Writers

In the fiction of the Pakistani-born novelist Bapsi Sidhwa and of the 2000 Pulitzer Prize winner Jhumpa Lahiri, one finds situations, characters and themes that are largely universal ones, rather than subjects unique to any particular ethnic group. A similar universal human appeal can be discerned in the work of emerging fiction writers Samrat Upadhyay, who was born in Nepal, and Akhil Sharma, who was born in India. Both Sharma and Upadhyay have already received recognition for their short stories in the past few years. Also noteworthy is Indian-born, Maryland-based Manil Suri, whose first novel, *The Death of Vishnu* (2001), has attracted considerable positive notice from readers and reviewers alike.

From the vast body of eighteenth-century historical documentation of the British in India, to the proliferation of Anglo-Indian fictions in the nineteenth and twentieth centuries, the narratives of English India or English South Asia are fraught with the idioms of dubiety, or a mode of cultural tale-telling that is neurotically conscious of its own self-censoring apparatus. While such narratives appear to claim a new preeminence of historical factuality over cultural allegory, they nonetheless illustrate that the functioning of language in a colonial universe is preternaturally dependent on the instability of its own facts. For colonial facts are vertiginous; they lack a recognizable cultural plot. They frequently tend to cohere around the master-myth that proclaims static lines of demarcation and disempowered culture between colonizer and colonized. If the 1980s turned out to be a decade of exhilarating political change around the world, the 1940s were a decade of death and devastation. To the horrors of the Holocaust, the killings and firebombings of the war in Europe and the Japanese outrages in East Asia, were added the massacres and atrocities that accompanied the partition of India in 1947, which took over one million lives, displaced thirteen million people and brutally treated millions more. One wonders how humanity survived at all. One measure of that survival is that tragedy gave birth to literature. In Europe, the experiences of ordinary individuals caught up in the trauma of history gone wrong resulted in exceptional books by extraordinary writers from Anne Frank and Eli Wiesel to Jerzy Kosinski and Gunther Grass.

In the Indian subcontinent the legacy is somewhat more ambiguous. The heirs of those who wrought the tragedy are still around; their triumphs are not universally mourned, and their hatreds still clog people's veins. These South Asian conflicts are among the themes of Bapsi Sidhwa's early novels. According to Niaz Zaman: "In *The Bride*, Sidhwa revealed her Pakistani identity by beginning with the train massacres; in *Ice-Candy-Man*, she would strengthen this identity even further by once more bringing in Indian atrocities committed in the Punjab" (*A Divided Legacy* 260).

Texas-based writer Bapsi Sidhwa began publishing in Pakistan before she immigrated to the United States. Bapsi Sidhwa was educated at home until the age of fifteen. She attended university in the Punjab, married, and had three children who are now adults. After visiting an isolated mountainous region in India and witnessing a village tragedy over a runaway bride, Sidhwa found the materials for her first novel, *The Bride* (1983). Sidhwa served on an advisory committee to former Pakistani Prime Minister Benazir Bhutto on Women's Development, and has been given numerous awards in Pakistan and elsewhere for her writing. One of her novels, *Cracking India* (1991), has been made into a film. Sidhwa has taught at Columbia University and the University of Houston, and is currently writer-in-residence at Mt. Holyoke.

If English India represents a discursive field that includes colonial and postcolonial narratives, it further represents an alternative to the troubled chronology of nationalism on the Indian subcontinent. In the first three decades after partition only a handful of writers—Saadat Hasan Manto in Urdu, Amrita Pritam in Punjabi, Khushwant Singh and Manohar Malgaokar in English—could be said to have produced memorable fiction about the catastrophe. When in more recent years South Asian novelists (led by Salman Rushdie) again returned to the period, they tended to prefer the grand historical sweep to the individual story. These writers have taken on the shaping forces of the era (1945–1950) rather than allowing a few ordinary lives to illuminate those forces. Bapsi Sidhwa is an intriguing exception. In several of her novels, she embodies the idioms of postcolonialism and its multiplicity of cultures with their divergent histories.

In her own fashion, Sidhwa has had to fight her own battles for independence. Like Lenny, her young Parsi narrator of *Cracking India*, she was a victim of polio, and because of her gender she was denied formal schooling until she was fourteen. She was married at nineteen and became a mother soon after. Therefore, she had to conceal her literary ambitions. These personal circumstances, this need to find an identity, led her to create characters who go through their journeys of initiation in search of a niche without the fiction becoming polemical. Her intent has always been to create women characters who speak for themselves, a characteristic of her writing that is similar to techniques of characterization employed by Mukherjee and Divakaruni.

The American title of her novel, *Cracking India*, which first appeared as *Ice-Candy-Man* (1988), alludes to partition and suggests another *Midnight's Children*. Simplicity is central to her depiction of characters. The story is not about partition, though that drama is certainly the backdrop; it is about "Lame Lenny," a little girl who has polio, who turns eight at a time when nobody feels like celebrating birthdays because of the pervasive ambiance. She is as concerned about the subtle physiological changes in her body as about the paradoxes of midnight. The novel is about Lenny's loss of innocence, about a world peopled with everyman characters called Electric-aunt and Slavesister and Oldhusband, about servants and laborers and artisans caught up in the inevitable sweep of history.

Lenny, like Sidhwa, is a Parsi, who are descendants of Zoroastrians who fled Muslim persecution in Persia in the eighth century and found refuge in the coastal state of Gujarat. The Parsis have thrived ever since, and because of their religion have kept out of the Hindu-Muslim sectarian divide. When partition came, the Parsis (like the Christians) stayed on the sidelines. They did not become victims of the mobs nor were they forced to flee across the newly created frontiers.

So Lenny and her family are not personally threatened but they live amid Hindus, Muslims, and Sikhs who are. Sidhwa's superb recreation of Lenny's early life richly evokes the colors, sounds and smells of pre-partition Lahore. Sidhwa has a particular talent for the larger-than-life eccentricities she portrayed so well in her first novel, *The Crow Eaters* (1978). But in *Cracking India* her most striking characters are the working-class adults little Lenny spends most of her time with: her Hindu nursemaid, Ayah; the gruffly paternal Muslim cook, Imam Din; the untouchable gardener, Har the Sikh; zoo attendant Sher Singh; and Ayah's Muslim admirers—a nameless masseur, the knife-sharpening Sharbat Khan, and the mercurial Ice-Candy-Man.

It is the suggestively *zaftig* Ayah, desired by every man, who is the focal point of the book. But looming over the narrative is the enigmatic shadow of Ice-Candy-Man, who undergoes transformations that dramatically prefigure those of the world around him. Through Lenny's eyes we see him as the eager popsicle vendor whose toes sneak under Ayah's sari early in the story; as the fake Sufi with copper wiring coiled around his neck and chest who declares that he is Allah's telephone (and calls Him with an invisible dial); as the fanatical mob leader who sickeningly betrays his love; and as the pimp-poet with amber eyes and oval face reciting Urdu verse to woo the woman he has destroyed. It is impossible not to see Ice-Candy-Man as a potential metaphor for society as well as for the inherent capriciousness of humanity.

Sidhwa sees beyond religious strife and its "symbols" to the poignant humanity of both fanatic and victim:

> And suddenly I become aware of religious differences. It is sudden. One day everybody is themselves—and the next day they are Hindu, Muslim, Sikh, Christian. People shrink, dwindling into symbols. Ayah is no longer my all-encompassing Ayah—she is also a token, a Hindu [*Cracking India* 101].

The intensely moving scene in which an inflamed Muslim mob comes to Lenny's house looking for Hindus is written with remarkable power and restraint. Ayah is forcibly taken away: "Four men stand pressed against her, propping her body upright, their lips stretched in triumphant grimaces" (*Cracking India* 195). *Cracking India* is a novel in which heartbreak coexists with slapstick, where awful jokes about forefathers and foreskins give way to descriptive prose of glowing beauty. The author's capacity for bringing an assortment of characters vividly to life leaves a lasting impression upon readers.

Remarkably, politics is not Sidhwa's forte. When her characters discuss the issues of the day, her deftness collapses in clichés and historical accuracy is sacrificed. In this seemingly realistic tale, Mahatma Gandhi's march to the sea protesting the British tax on salt is misplaced by a decade and a half, and Sidhwa uses her authorial authority to inform the reader that the British favored Nehru over Jinnah, and since Nehru was a Kashmiri, India was given Kashmir. These statements are not simply wrong (the Maharajah of Kashmir acceded to India a year after partition); they undermine Sidhwa's narrator. Nor, where dialogue is concerned, does one expect a writer of Sidhwa's quality to have sturdy Punjabi peasants talking like Bengali art critics. However, even these shortcomings reveal a fine sensibility immersed in the assumption that politics only matters because it affects human beings. In depicting the historic events of partition through the perceptions of a polio-ridden child, a girl who tries to wrench out her tongue because it is unable to lie, *Cracking India* is a memorable book, one that confirms Sidhwa's position of eminence among Pakistan's English-language novelists.

The Bride (1983) is Sidhwa's second published novel and probably her most controversial. (It was really her first novel although it was published after *The Crow Eaters*). The controversy stems from the underlying political fabric of the novel, the politics of the late 1970s and early 1980s, and from the female characters who, in search of their own identities, defy tradition and in the process go against the entire political-minded authority. In this sense *The Bride* has a structural similarity with Rushdie's *Shame*, which seeks to represent what was until recently a veiled segment of history in Pakistan—the 1978 execution of its former president, Zulfikar Ali Bhutto. Even though *The Bride* does not contain the cultural complexity of *Shame*, in essence it is dealing with the same issues. The technique in Sidhwa's case is to create characters who begin as everyman figures who, in the quest for their destiny, become icons and heroes and ultimately larger than life.

The Bride is Sidhwa's only novel that does not revolve around her own Parsi community. The plot begins amidst the setting of the train massacres, from which Qasim adopts a lost little girl, Zaitoon, in memory of his own lost child. Sidhwa paints a graphic and grisly scene of the massacre:

> Now the mob runs toward the train with lighted flares. Qasim sees the men clearly. They are Sikhs. Tall, crazed men wave swords. A cry: "Bole so Nihal," and the answering roar, "Sat Sri Akal!" Torches unevenly light the scene and Qasim watches the massacre as in a cinema. An eerie clamour rises. Sounds of firing explode above agonized shrieks [*The Bride* 27–28].

This is almost the mirror image of the Sikh refugee's heartrending tale in Mehta's *The Ledge Between the Streams*, an encapsulation of tragic moments in history, of postcolonial mistakes from which South Asia has never made a complete political recovery. It is this terrifying moment of history that changes Zaitoon's life forever.

The Bride is essentially the story of the young woman Zaitoon and her symbolic journey, in which she accompanies her father Qasim to the home of her betrothed Sakhi, who, like her father, was once of the hill people. During the journey she comes into contact with Ashiq Hussain, the truck driver who ferries Qasim and Zaitoon to Dubair in the hill country. The journey is more than an eye-opener for the teenaged Zaitoon. Her inexplicable feelings in the proximity of probably the first male she has known outside her immediate family affect her strongly.

Sidhwa goes into some detail in depicting the consummation of Zaitoon's marriage to Sakhi. Zaitoon has accepted her lover's hand on her breasts, not as foreplay but as the final capitulation. Brought up in a vacuum, she did not think of sex as good or bad—it simply did not exist. The love scenes contain vivid poetic details that suggest the influence of D.H. Lawrence (*The Bride* 163–164).

The apparent dichotomy between this vision of love and her husband's insane jealousy and hateful demeanor the very next moment, leads Zaitoon to make the very first decision in her life. She decides to leave Sakhi. This act of defiance, which her father does not understand or support, completes Zaitoon's emergence into womanhood/adulthood and originates from her growing realization that a marriage is a relationship founded on the bed of mutual respect and equal partnership. In the society of the hill-country this concept is blasphemy, sacrilegious, unthinkable. As Zaitoon sees the real Sakhi emerge from his physical magnificence into a cruel wife-abuser whose physical abuse and mental manipulation are intolerable, she is forced to take the step of leaving Sakhi as the only escape possible—she must run away.

Zaitoon's flight from the village and her attempts to evade Sakhi, her passion for life that helps her survive the hills and have a chance at a "normal" life, complete her process of self-realization. She emerges in a sense like "Sita" before the fire, unashamed of her decision as a new woman, liberated from the bonds of a repressive relationship and a culture which condones the total subjugation of her body and soul by her husband.

Against the stark background of the action, the ultra-orthodox society and the context of life in Pakistan, Sidhwa's Zaitoon is the woman who is different from the crowd in essence—she respects herself. In this Zaitoon is typical of the female characters Bapsi Sidhwa has created, like Lenny and Feroza—even like Carol in *The Bride*, who is redeemed by her defense of Zaitoon and her realization that she matters as little to her lover as Zaitoon did to the tribesmen of the hills. And Carol emerges stronger as she decides to leave Farukh and return home to the United States.

Whether Bapsi Sidhwa's new woman will make her mark on the stifling ambience of South Asian culture does not seem to be the issue. What is at stake seems to be the conscience of an entire society, which, to transform, must retain its base value and yet change and begin to consider all its citizens as equals in the eyes of the law as well as in the hearts and minds of the people, not only in practice but in essence.

Bapsi Sidhwa's fourth novel, *An American Brat* (1993), is about Feroza Ginwalla, a descendant of the Junglewalla clan portrayed in *The Crow Eaters* (1978). But whereas the latter details the rags-to-riches life of Faredoon Junglewalla and her family in pre-partition Pakistan, *An American*

Brat is a coming-of-age story, an initiation tale of how America appears to a new arrival—and an exploration of the impact it has on her as she searches for her own identity.

Feroza, a sixteen-year-old Parsi woman from Lahore, is shipped off to the United States, ostensibly to ward off the effects of an ultra-orthodox Islamic environment prevalent in Pakistan in the late 1970s. She stays with her uncle Manek, a graduate student at MIT who, although only six years her senior, is a crafty veteran of life in America. It is mainly because of him that her planned three-month visit turns into at least a four-year stay. While attending college in Denver, Feroza falls in love with David, a Jewish student whose family is as orthodox as hers. After learning the couple intends to marry, Feroza's mother sets out for America to make Feroza change her mind. The battles fought by mother, daughter and prospective son-in-law are handled deftly, illuminating the difficulties that arise when culture takes a seat before the search for self-definition.

The quest for self-definition is at the heart of *An American Brat*. A case in point occurs near the end of the novel when, in a fit of post-natal depression, Aban, Manek's wife, declares that everything she desires is in Karachi (*Brat* 316). This quest is also reinforced by Feroza's own sojourn — her pitiful breakup with David, her mother Zareen's own assessment that her daughter would probably choose to return to her roots. And when, at the end of the novel, she muses about her fate if she were to marry a non-Parsi, she realizes that her religion is one she carries in her heart (*Brat* 317). Her realization indicates a new practicality in a view of life that still adheres to its basic principles. In spite of the lack of resolution to her problems, it is a new Feroza who develops in *An American Brat* as a result of her coming-to-America experiences.

Unlike Sidhwa's characters and plots where an element of social critique always remains latent, the fiction of Jhumpa Lahiri contains the writing of an observer whose keen eye penetrates into the conflicts within the psyches of the individuals whose stories she narrates. Lahiri has a talent for developing characters to the fullest extent possible within the scope of the postmodern short story. And refreshingly, despite all of the poststructuralists' distrust of language, Lahiri's fiction has a beginning, middle and an end.

On April 10, 2000, Lahiri was awarded the Pulitzer Prize for fiction, the first South Asian winner of this coveted award whose previous recipients have included names as luminous as John Steinbeck, Ernest Hemingway, Saul Bellow, William Faulkner, John Updike, Norman Mailer, and Pearl S. Buck. Perhaps the most important aspect of Lahiri's recognition is its placing of South Asian fiction amongst the canon of American literature. Lahiri's work achieves the movement away from subjects uniquely ethnic to subjects universally human in her first collection, *The Interpreter of Maladies* (1999).

Born in 1967 in London, Lahiri grew up in Rhode Island. She has a B.A. from Barnard College in English Literature, and M.A. and Ph.D. from Boston University. The title story of her collection was selected for both the O. Henry Award and the *Best American Short Stories 2000*. In the tradition of earlier South Asian writers Mehta and Jhabvala, Lahiri was included in *The New Yorker* summer fiction issue of 1999 as "one of the 20 best writers under the age of 40."

The Interpreter of Maladies contains two types of fiction: a few stories dealing with Indian characters in an Indian setting and others set in the New World among first- and second-generation diasporic South Asians. While there are no cataclysmic events chronicled in the stories, over and over again Lahiri depicts characters who come to terms with their internal conflicts as they face changes they must consider both within and without in trying to understand themselves. Thus, in "A Temporary Matter," a young urban professional couple, Shoba and Shukumar, realize that they no longer love one another. This realization comes to them in stages after their baby is born dead, and their disillusionment is clearly manifest as they tell each other things that they previously had not revealed:

> Shoba looked at him now, her face contorted with sorrow. He had cheated on a college exam, ripped a picture of a woman out of a magazine. He had returned a sweater and got drunk in the middle of the day instead. These were the things he told her. He had held his son, who had known life only within her, against his chest in a darkened room in an unknown wing of the hospital.... She came back to the table and sat down, and after a moment Shukumar joined her. They wept together, for the things they now knew ["A Temporary Matter" 22].

The couple's loss of love is symbolized by their weeping together.

Just as the drifting apart of Shoba and Shukumar could be the predicament of any couple anywhere in this age, the adultery of Mrs. Das as confessed to Mr. Kapasi in "The Interpreter of Maladies," has elements of classic Madame Bovaryesque discontent. Marrying her schooldays sweetheart, housebound with a small child, Mrs. Das conceives a child in a single afternoon's affair with her husband's friend who is a short-term house guest. Years later, the Das family is on vacation in India on a sightseeing trip. Their tour guide, Mr. Kapasi, also has another job — as an interpreter at a physician's office translating from different Indian languages between the physician and his numerous patients. In a sense "The Interpreter of Maladies," Mr. Kapasi is aware of the lack of love and sexual fulfillment in his own marriage. He also senses the latent discontents of Mrs. Das and her almost defiant attitude to her husband. When Mrs. Das takes an interest in him and asks for his address so that she can mail him photographs of the tour, he fantasizes a long correspondence with her. Of course, she suddenly tells him about her adulterous episode when her son Bobby gets close to the wild monkeys. But the monkeys strike Bobby with a stick, bringing the tour to an abrupt end. As she becomes the concerned mother, Mrs. Das unwittingly puts an end to Mr. Kapasi's fantasy of a long letter-writing friendship:

> "Poor Bobby," Mrs. Das said. "Come here a second. Let Mommy fix your hair." Again she reached into her straw bag, this time for her hairbrush.... When she whipped out the hairbrush, the slip of paper with Mr. Kapasi's address on it fluttered away in the wind. No one but Mr. Kapasi noticed. He watched as it rose, carried higher and higher by the breeze, into the trees where the monkeys now sat, solemnly observing the scene below. Mr. Kapasi observed it too, knowing that this was the picture of the Das family he would preserve forever in his mind ["Interpreter" 68–69].

Thus Mr. Kapasi is returned to his chronic lonesome condition.

Over and over again, Lahiri reminds us that pain and separation are recurring features of the human condition. In "Mrs. Sen's," the protagonist Miranda breaks off her liaison with her married lover, Dev, when a little boy, Robin, tells her the story of his father's adultery and his mother's anguish. (108–109) In the story, the point of view is that of a boy named Eliot who is placed with a number of babysitters after school. He forms a friendship with one, Mrs. Sen, the wife of a visiting professor from India. The arrangement concludes abruptly when Mrs. Sen is involved in a minor auto accident: She drives with Eliot as a passenger and without her license. Thus Eliot loses his interesting friend:

> He said she was resting, though when Eliot had gone to the bathroom he'd heard her crying. His mother was satisfied with the arrangement, and in a sense, she confessed to Eliot as they drove home, she was relieved. It was the last afternoon Eliot spent with Mrs. Sen or with any baby-sitter. From then on his mother gave him a key, which he wore on a string around his neck. He was to call the neighbors in case of an emergency, and to let himself into the beach house after school ["Mrs. Sen's" 135].

Relationships and personality differences present endless possibilities for Lahiri in her fictional plots. In "This Blessed House," Sanjeev, who is raised in the Hindu religion, wishes that his newlywed wife Twinkle would not display the Christian artifacts that she keeps discovering in the home they have bought and moved into. Finally, on the night of the housewarming party, she takes all the guests into the attic on a treasure hunt to find a solid silver bust of Christ weighing about thirty pounds. The statue becomes a symbol of Sanjeev's and Twinkle's differences, differences that couples must reconcile within themselves if they are to stay together:

> She took a breath, raised her eyebrows, crossed her fingers. "Would you mind terribly if we displayed it on the mantel? Just for tonight? I know you hate it."
> He did hate it. He hated its immensity, and its flawless, polished surface, and its undeniable value. He hated that it was in his house, and that he owned it. Unlike some other things they'd found, this contained dignity, solemnity, beauty even. But to his surprise these qualities made him hate it all the more. Most of all he hated it because Twinkle loved it ["Blessed House" 156–157].

In "The Third and Final Continent," one of the three short stories that won a National Magazine Award for *The New Yorker*'s summer 1999 fiction issue, Lahiri creates a first-person narrator, an Indian immigrant who comes to the U.S. as a librarian for M.I.T. In *Best American Short Stories 2000*, Lahiri informs readers that this plot is based upon a real episode in her own father's early life (356–357). This short story encapsulates the protagonist's arranged marriage, his good feelings towards his wife, his short stay as a tenant in the home of the hundred-year-old Mrs. Croft in Cambridge, as stages in the life of a South Asian immigrant who views himself as a survivor:

> In my son's eyes I see the ambition that had first hurled me across the world. In a few years he will graduate and pave his way, alone and unprotected. But I remind myself that he has a father who is still living, a mother who is happy and strong. Whenever he is discouraged, I tell him that if I can survive on three continents, then there is no obstacle he cannot conquer ["Third and Final Continent" 197–198].

In any sense, South Asian fiction is like the protagonist of "The Third and Final Continent," in that it encompasses Asian and European influences and blossoms in the New World. The fiction of Nepali-born Samrat Upadhyay is representative of this migration across continents. Upadhyay received his Ph.D. in English from the University of Hawaii, and now teaches at Baldwin-Wallace College. He has received awards for his short fiction, and his story "The Good Shopkeeper" appeared in *Best American Short Stories 1999*. Upadhyay claims, "I never work with plot when I write a short story; I start with a strong image or a mood, then follow the impulse, letting language and characters dictate the story line" (*Best American Short Stories 1999*).

In "The Good Shopkeeper," Upadhyay's character development cuts across social classes, depicting Pramod, a middle-class man in contemporary Nepal who suddenly becomes unemployed. Unemployment brings feelings of isolation and alienation. A proper husband, father, and provider before he lost his job, Pramod seeks companionship outside his social class with a servant girl. This friendship becomes an extra-marital affair: "He didn't know what he thought of her, except that there was an inevitability to all of this—something he had sensed the moment he first talked to her in the park" ("The Good Shopkeeper" 344). At the end of the story, Pramod agrees to his wife's suggestion of becoming self-employed as a shopkeeper. Thus, Upadhyay clearly demonstrates the effects of unemployment on the protagonist's self-esteem and his marriage, thereby reminding readers that the negative effects of unemployment are part of universal human experience.

Like Samrat Upadhyay, Akhil Sharma successfully develops both male and female viewpoints with stark realism. Sharma states that he reads the classics, and that knowledge of history broadens the imagination (Reeder 3). For a relatively young writer, Sharma's knowledge of history and of human character is impressive. Sharma was born in Delhi, India, in 1971. He received a B.A. in public policy from Princeton University, held a creative writing fellowship at Stanford University, and worked as a screenwriter for Universal Studios. After graduating from Harvard Law School, Sharma is now an investment banker. His stories have appeared in *The Best American Short Stories* anthologies, the *O. Henry Award Winners* anthology, *The Atlantic Monthly*, *The New Yorker*, *The Quarterly*, and *Fiction*.

If Upadhyay creates the pain of unemployment, Akhil Sharma creates the pain of a lonely retirement in "Cosmopolitan," anthologized in *Best America Short Stories 1998*. In this short story Sharma depicts two lonely middle-aged neighbors who drift into sexual encounters and then separate temporarily. The story shows the isolation of retirement for Gopal Maurya, whose wife has left him to join a religious order in India and whose grown daughter is hardly ever in touch with him. At the end, as Gopal decides to resume seeing Helen Shaw, he realizes that being middle-aged and lonely has in a sense freed them both from the romantic expectations of youth: "This is who we are, he thought—dusty, corroded, and dented from our voyages, with our unflagging hearts rattling on inside....Why should we need anything else to fall in love?" ("Cosmopolitan" 69).

Sharma's first novel, *An Obedient Father* (2000), also uses the point of view of an older man whose wife is dead, but whose widowed daughter and granddaughter live with him. The setting is Delhi in the 1980s. The title itself is ironic because the father's "obedience" to his daughter's wishes leads to his death. The novel is a dark tale of moral and political corruption in modern India. At the center of the novel are incest, rape, guilt, shame, and murder. Set in the slums of the old city of Delhi, Sharma's novel paints a sinister picture of political corruption and moral decay in India's capital during the late 1980s. In interviews, Sharma states that he has remained familiar with the real aspects of life in India because of frequent trips taken with his parents while he was growing up (Hogan 1).

The protagonist, Ram Karan, molested and raped his daughter Anita when she was twelve years old. Karan supplements his income as a petty civil servant by taking bribes on behalf of political parties. The interior monologues of Karan and Anita have a stark and raw quality that leave an indelible impression of evil and corruption. The only positive character is young Asha. Asha is sent away to America with Anita's sister Kusum, who is married to a white American. One hopes that with this departure Asha leaves the decadence of Delhi behind her. Like Chitra Banerjee Divakaruni, Sharma does not flinch from satirizing the social and moral evils of contemporary South Asia.

Sharma's tragicomic tale of incest and corruption paints a startling picture of working-class life in postcolonial India. Sharma's satiric method links him to the tradition of novelists such as the 2001 Nobel Prize winner V.S. Naipaul and Commonwealth Writers Award winner Shashi Tharoor. Ram Karan and his dysfunctional family may enjoy as lasting a place in postcolonial fiction as the unforgettable caricatures of the Tulsi household in Naipaul's *A House for Mr. Biswas*. In his Nobel lecture on December 7, 2001, Naipaul mentions that his fiction depicts geographical "areas of darkness" within or without the individual. Sharma's novel depicts dark areas and evil places within the psyche. A striking feature of the novel is the uncertainty about who is the protagonist and who is the antagonist. In his use of this fictional technique, Sharma reminds readers of Toni Morrison.

There are three discernible layers of corruption in Sharma's novel. The three levels of corruption in *An Obedient Father* are as monstrous and destructive as Satan's three faces in Dante's *Inferno*. The first level is that of the state, the Mafia-like local government that indulges in bribery and crime, even murder, as routine process. The second level is the incest, as moral corruption within another valued social institution, the family. The third level is that of the individual—the corruption of Ram Karan, of his daughter Anita, and of her vengeance upon him.

The novel is structured in the form of twelve sectional narratives. The point of view shifts in each section with carefully crafted parallelism and contrast becoming evident as different characters reveal their individual versions of the same episode. These contrasting points of view in the sectional narratives constitute the novelist's unique method of character development. In the first section, the protagonist Ram Karan narrates the daily routines of his present life as a petty civil servant. In section two, there is Anita's flashback after her father's death, a sudden disruption of chronological sequence. The dead mother is characterized through the memories of the daughter and the husband. Section three moves several decades back in time with Ram Karan's flashbacks to his childhood and adolescence. The fourth section allows Ram Karan to dwell on political intrigues and corruption: in the context of the 1980s, the Congress Party and the Bharatiya Janata Party are both equally corrupt.

Sections six through ten bring to life the daily stresses of Ram Karan's life which consist of tensions at work and his fear of Anita as he befriends his granddaughter Asha. These conflicts are out in the open when Anita accuses him of having sexual designs on Asha. Then Anita warns Asha in very crude terms. Anita also tells the story of her rape to her deceased mother's sister and extended family.

In section eleven, Anita gets her revenge by feeding her father rich and heavily seasoned food and taking his heart medications away. Ram Karan is either excessively greedy or suicidal in that he keeps eating the rich food she serves, and has a heart attack.

Thus the roles of protagonist and antagonist are switched by Sharma's plot structure. Anita even keeps Karan locked in his room. A wicked combination of psychological torture, lack of medicine, and the fat-filled food ultimately kills Ram Karan. Hence the ironic title *An Obedient Father*: Karan's obedience is his destruction and Anita's worst wish fulfillment.

The novel's closure has the adolescent Asha leaving the slums of Delhi for America. The ending is disappointing in that Asha's escape is physical. Readers are left to ponder the emotional baggage that she will permanently carry with her to the New World.

Just as Asha will carry her inner "area of darkness" to the New World, Sharma's novel explores the "areas of darkness" within and without the individual. Ram Karan's narratives almost give the reader a sympathetic point of view. Sharma's art allows the reader to enter into the motives behind Ram Karan's terrible experiences, his acts of child molestation and incest, as the shifts in point of view and flashbacks allow the reader to observe the progression of Ram Karan's evil desires: "I believed at that time that it was my unavoidable doom as much as lust which made me tell Anita to come sleep in my room again. But it was probably simply that I did not actually believe that I would ever be discovered, for I could not imagine the world after I had been caught" (*An Obedient Father* 96).

Ram Karan has vivid memories of his early encounters with child prostitutes before he married his wife Radha, with whom he had three children:

> In Bombay I slept with a child. An acquaintance told me about the girl, that she was thirteen. I went looking for her the evening of the same day I heard of her. I imagine this means something. But at that point I was not actually interested in children. What I found exciting was the idea of doing something altogether different from what had become banal to me [*An Obedient Father* 78].

Ram Karan remembers exactly how, as a middle-aged man, he first molested, then raped his twelve-year-old daughter Anita:

> But for four or five nights there was the same horror. The details of what we did, Anita holding her cries in and breathing as though there were sand in her lungs, were so terrible that whenever I finished I felt as if I were swallowing my tongue. Yet each night Anita sat on the edge of her cot and I closed the door and switched off the light before turning around [*An Obedient Father* 97].

Sharma's prose has graphic details that tend to make the reader flinch.

From the memories of his entirely corrupt sexuality to his routine acceptance of bribes as a petty civil servant, it is not easy for Ram Karan to live with himself. Yet Ram Karan prides himself on being an excellent provider and is later able to appease Anita's wrath with large sums of money.

The largest thematic question that Sharma's novel poses is broader than the subject of corruption and moral decay in postcolonial India. That question is whether there can be any solutions to the problem of moral decay in an environment where the *ethos* itself is totally corrupt. The novel is surprisingly successful in generating sympathy for both Ram Karan, corrupt government official and incestuous father, and for Anita, widowed guardian of an eight-year-old daughter and financially dependent on the very father who raped her. In the unexpected turns of the plot, Anita blackmails and murders Ram Karan. The work is innovative in that Ram Karan and Anita in turn serve as both protagonist and antagonist within the novel's carefully orchestrated shifting points of view.

The Death of Vishnu (2001), Manil Suri's first novel, rapidly made best-seller lists. Suri is a Maryland-based Indian-born professor of mathematics who has taken up fiction writing with success. The novel is set in a slumlike Bombay (Mumbai) apartment building and its events take on a surrealistic quality. Various strands of narrative about the building's residents are woven around the central character, Vishnu of the title, who lies dying. In the author's note to the novel, Suri writes:

> Although the persons and events depicted in this novel are fictional, the central character was informed by a man named Vishnu who lived on the steps of the apartment building in which I grew up. He died in August 1994 on the same landing he had occupied for many years [Author's note n. p.].

Vishnu is an alcoholic who lives on the landing of a lower-middle-class apartment building in Bombay, the largest city in western India. Suri's narrative has a factual and sociological basis in that Bombay is an overpopulated megalopolis with a chronic shortage of suitable housing for lower income groups. Rents are also astronomical for working-class Bombay residents. In this novel two families, the Asranis and the Pathaks, share the same kitchen. The men of these two households are on good terms because they do not have to work together. However, their wives are permanently on quarreling terms, with the kitchen as the center of their territorial strife.

In structure, Suri's novel is a dark comedy compiled from a series of interior monologues by different characters including Vishnu himself. Manil Suri's style of writing verges on caricature. The style and organization of the novel is reminiscent of Akhil Sharma's *An Obedient Father*. Although Suri himself is a first-generation South Asian immigrant, *The Death of Vishnu* has no links with the New World immigrant experience. Suri writes a narrative of a long-lost past in Bombay based upon his own experiences.

Suri excels at comic characterization. In the residents of the apartment building, Suri creates unforgettable comic character types such as Mrs. Pathak and Kavita Asrani. Mrs. Pathak's social aspirations are embodied in her so-called "kitty party," which rapidly becomes a fiasco when none of the building's residents are willing to share the costs of ambulance and medical treatment for the dying Vishnu. The arrival of the ambulance and the squabble between the neighbors ends the "kitty party" very swiftly. Thus Suri satirizes the "kitty party," a popular social event among urban middle-class women in India.

In addition to the feud between the Asranis and the Pathaks, Suri develops the subplot of the elopement of eighteen-year-old Kavita Asrani with the Muslim neighbor's son Salim. Suri develops in dramatic detail the teenagers' romance aided by Vishnu, the actual elopement of Kavita and Salim, and the couple's breakup. Kavita leaves Salim because he fails her in her bourgeois expectations of married life: He plans to be an auto mechanic; she does not want to be married to an auto mechanic.

On the other side of the comic episode of Kavita and Salim is the Hindu-Muslim riot that is sparked off by Kavita's elopement. The riot changes the comic scenario into a grim one when Salim's mother suffers a serious head injury when a mob attacks Salim's parents in their apartment following the young couple's disappearance. The episode exposes the underlying bigotry of lower-class life in Bombay.

The novel also develops the religious crisis of Mr. Jalal, who wanders from the stern ways of Islam into what his wife considers to be the superstitious and mystical beliefs of Hinduism. Confused in his system of beliefs, Mr. Jalal even spends the night sleeping on the landing with the unconscious Vishnu, who has lost control of his bowels.

The interior monologues turn poetic and emotive in their narrative of the various romantic memories of Vishnu, who had loved the prostitute Padnini. Vishnu's memories are evocative of a life of lost opportunities and unrequited desires. Ironically, Vishnu—loser, drunk, and bum—ascends into heaven while riot conditions descend upon the apartment building.

Overall, *The Death of Vishnu* is a satiric capsule of Indian urban life where the death of Vishnu (named after the Hindu god) emerges as a contemporary version of "Dead Are All the Gods." The existentialist theme of the book and the absurdist turn of events in the riot suggest the postmodern influences on Suri's writing. A degree of comic relief is present in the bride-viewing scenes where Kavita meets a prospective candidate for a traditional arranged marriage.

Without being sexist, Manil Suri creates realistic women characters who seem to be mercenary and scheming. Some of Suri's satire borders upon harshness as he depicts women who are very controlling of their husbands. The ancient South Asian practice of arranged marriages is held up under a naked light as it were. In this characteristic, Suri displays similarities to Bharati Mukherjee and Chitra Divakaruni. However, Suri's fictional world is not devoid of romantic love. In the apartment building there also lives Vinod Taneja, whose story provides a welcome relief to the loveless marriages in the building. Vinod Taneja is a recluse in retirement. He lives with the memory of his beloved wife Sheetal, who died of cancer.

Suri's existentialist vision of living and dying in urban India is reminiscent of William Faulkner's *As I Lay Dying*, which uses a country setting. Also, Suri's depiction of the extreme contrasts among the residents of Bombay is echoed in the fiction of Vikram Chandra and Rohinton Mistry.

6

Another World, Another Time: The Fiction of Anita Desai, Amitav Ghosh, and Other Contemporary Novelists

In the last decade, the American reading public and the North American publishing scene have witnessed the swift growth of novels and short fiction by immigrant and visiting writers from South Asia—works that continue to focus upon South Asian characters in South Asian settings and contexts, though the plots sometimes include North America contexts, as in Amitrav Ghosh's *The Calcutta Chromosome* and Vikram Chandra's *Red Earth and Pouring Pain*. Ghosh and Chandra are both examples of expatriate Indian writers who are recent immigrants to the American professoriate. In this group of writers from South Asia, the artist is physically in America but the artist's psyche remains in the Old World, envisioning complex characters, plots, and themes in South Asian contexts.

The types of novels created by this group of writers include genres as different from one another as fantasies, historical novels, science fiction, family dramas, and voluminous cross-generational sagas such as *A Suitable Boy* by Vikram Seth. All five writers discussed in this chapter have large audiences among the educated middle-class reading public in India. These novelists include Anita Desai, Amitav Ghosh, Vikram Chandra, Vikram Seth, and Manju Kapur.

Large canvases and massive novels have been popular in the realm of Indian vernacular literature since the beginning of the nineteenth century. Novelists writing in Indian languages were often inspired by the sweep of Victorian British fiction. The serialized novel published in literary magazines continued to be a popular form until recent times. With the world's largest film industry in Bollywood, India produces numerous feature films that tend to run almost four hours. Indian television serials have multistrand plots and numerous characters. In the light of the prevalence of large canvases in the visual media, one may infer that the novelists are writing for similar audiences.

The first of the group of five popular contemporary novelists from India to achieve recognition was Anita Desai. Desai is currently writer-in-residence at the Massachusetts Institute of Technology. Born on January 24, 1937, Anita Desai's father was Indian and her mother was German. Most of her early life was spent in New Delhi, and her fictional characters and settings continue to use New Delhi and its suburbs. In early childhood, Desai spoke German and Hindi, the languages of her parents. Like most children in modern urban India, Desai learned English when she started school. Learning to read and write in English, a language that continues to be a common medium of classroom instruction and business communication in India, Desai started to write her early fiction in English. It may be observed that writing in English gives Indian writers access to a much larger reading public both inside and outside of India compared to the more limited audiences who read fiction in the different Indian languages. Desai herself has commented, "I think it had a tremendous effect that the first thing you saw written and the first thing you ever read was English. It seemed to me the language of books. I just went on writing because I always wanted to belong to this world of books" (Julik 1).

Desai studied at the University of Delhi where she earned a B.A. in English, graduating with honors. She married Ashrin Desai on December 15, 1958, and started publishing fiction soon after her marriage. Desai has four children: Rahul, Tani, Arjun and Kiran. Among her appointments to professional organizations are membership on the Advisory Board for English, membership in the American Academy of Arts and Letters, and Fellow of the Royal Society of Literature. Her academic appointments have been at Mt. Holyoke, Smith, and Girton College at Cambridge University. Desai received international recognition before she relocated to the United States. Among her many literary awards are the 1978 National Academy of Letters Award for *Fire on the Mountain*, the Guardian Prize for children's fiction (1983) for *The Village by the Sea*, the Literary Lion Award (1993), and several prestigious fellowships at Cambridge. Anita Desai has a prolific publication record with fourteen works of fiction to her credit: *Cry, the Peacock* (1963), *Voice in the City* (1965), *Bye-Bye, Blackbird* (1968), *Fire on the Mountain* (1977), *Games at Twilight* (1978), *Where Shall We Go This Summer?* (1975), *The Peacock Garden* (1974), *Clear Light of Day* (1980 and 2000), *The Village by the Sea* (1982), *In Custody* (1984), *Baumgartner's Bombay* (1989), *Journey to Ithaca* (1995), and *Fasting, Feasting* (1999 and 2000).

6. Another World, Another Time

The two novels in the most recent editions, *Clear Light of Day* (first edition 1980) and *Fasting, Feasting* (first edition 1999) contain most of the major characteristics of Desai's fiction in their depiction of South Asian women and men coping with the multi-faceted dimensions of change within family life, within contemporary society, and between cultures. Desai's primary focus through her career has been on women characters whose self-development has often been suppressed within the traditional patriarchal structures of the Indian family. Desai brings to life the inner dilemma and inner conflicts of women characters that traditional Indian society has to an extent disregarded. The female protagonists of Desai's fiction seem to trace their descent lines to the anti-heroes of modern and postmodern fiction. Desai's art aims to uncover "the truth that is nine tenths of the iceberg that lies submerged beneath the one-tenth visible portion we call Reality" (Julik 2).

Clear Light of Day (1980, 2000) revolves around the lives of three siblings and has been described by Fawzia Afzal-Khan as "Chekovian" (83). In it Desai replicates the slow pace of life in her native Delhi in the nineteen forties, recreating the transition in India's capital from colonial into postcolonial times.

In *Clear Light of Day* the mother dies of a stroke and the father dies in an auto accident, leaving two daughters and a son. Of the two sisters, Tara marries Bakul and Bim remains single. The point of view of the book is that of Bim, the spinster sister. The youngest of the family is the brother Raja, a tubercular college student. The ailing Raja is an aspiring Hindu poet with liberal views on Hindu-Muslim unity. As Chelva Kanaganayakam points out,

> Thus, in *Clear Light of Day*, Raja's sudden illness during the Partition riots serves the metonymic function of pointing to a larger disease in the body politic. Given the naïve romanticism of Raja, his sickness becomes a parody of Gandhi's fast to end the riots [*Counterrealism* 86].

Clear Light of Day contains several minor characters whose stories bring to life the nineteen-forties setting in Delhi. The family relationships mirror the way of life of the Indian extended family, a common theme for Indian fiction writers. The relationships in this novel, and even the types of characters, are reworked and developed in Desai's more recent novel, *Fasting, Feasting*. An example is the aunt Mira Masi, who moves in with the orphaned sisters and brother: The same name, Mira Masi, surfaces in *Fasting, Feasting*. Kanaganayakam suggests that

> Marginalized by tradition, class, and gender, Mira, ironically, recalls the lover of Krishna. In a novel where the names of the main char-

acters—Bim, Tara, Baba—are deliberately stripped of connotative meanings, the intertextuality implied by Mira acquires a special significance [*Counterrealism* 90].

In *Fasting, Feasting* (1999) the only connection with America and American life is the narrative of Arun, the youngest child and only son of an Indian family who comes to attend college in Massachusetts. Arun lives in the summer with the Patton family. Mrs. Patton loves having Arun as a houseguest. She turns vegetarian to keep him company, though her vegetarian dishes are quite inedible to Arun. The Patton family is somewhat strange in that the son Rod is a fitness freak, and the daughter Melanie is a bulimic who is sent to an institution for recovery. The head of the household, Mr. Patton, likes his red meat. Desai's portrayal of the Pattons is tinged with gentle satire. Despite the friendliness of the Pattons, Arun is happy to return to his dormitory from his experiences of family life in a suburban Massachusetts home.

Desai handles cultural differences with understanding, sensitivity, and balance. The Pattons are perhaps less dysfunctional than Arun's own family in a provincial town somewhere in northern India. The novel's title comes from the "fasting feasting" point of view of Uma, Arun's sister who serves as caregiver to elderly parents who will not allow her a life of her own. Uma is an epileptic. As a girl she is a poor student who is taken out of Catholic school because of failing grades to help with the family's new baby, Arun. Arun is a child born late in the parents' marriage. Arun's older siblings are two sisters, of whom Uma is the plain one.

The plight of Uma is one of Desai's most telling narratives of the oppression of women within the intensely patriarchal structure of the Indian extended family. Homebound and deprived of an education because of her academic deficiencies, Uma's future is planned by her parents in terms of a traditional arranged marriage. But this traditional woman's career also evades the "fasting" Uma. At first Uma's father arranges a marriage for her with a prospective groom who defrauds the parents of her dowry. After the financial losses of this episode, the second attempt to arrange Uma's wedding actually results in a marriage to a man who turns out to be a bigamist. Soon after the ceremony the bridegroom leaves Uma with his mother and family, returning to his wife in another town.

When Uma's father learns of the husband's deception, he reclaims part of her dowry and takes her back to live at home. The marriage is legally annulled. Left with no skills to earn a living, doomed to a single life in the conservative society of northern India where divorced women are not considered eligible single women, Uma is fated to become the family's permanent housekeeper. She remains on the sidelines while Aruna, her pretty sister, marries a successful man. Ironically, Aruna is to spend the rest of her life nagging her husband and children, providing a clear contrast to the quiet and uneventful days of Uma's life with her parents.

The parallelism and contrast in Desai's art of characterization and plot construction are very distinct. A stronger contrast to the lives of Uma and Aruna is developed in the tale of their cousin Anamika, once accepted to Oxford University as a student but not sent there because she was given in a traditional Indian arranged marriage by her parents. Poor Anamika's household and in-laws have transformed her into a house slave. Finally, after twenty-five years of marriage, Anamika is burned to death under very suspicious circumstances. Anamika's death carries a powerful social message as it is a reminder of a long history of suspicious deaths in northern India over domestic disputes and marriage dowry portions. Anamika is possibly a victim of homicide like other homicides of women by burning, a social problem that has continued to plague both urban and rural community life in northern India in the last decades.

Desai's *Fasting, Feasting* contains a significant degree of social satire. The novel encapsulates the emptiness of provincial life with an emphasis on the boredom and horror of the lives of Indian women bound by patriarchal tradition in a permanent subordinate status. The novel brings out the double vision and hypocrisy of outdated social practices whereby, despite the legal availability of divorce and annulments, marriages continue to be regarded as indissoluble. In contrast to the married woman Anamika, who is probably a homicide victim, the divorced Uma may actually have a better and safer life—Desai's ultimate irony of women's lives and marriage in the context of traditional Indian society. Afzal-Khan summarizes Desai's stance thus:

> Anita Desai's position as a postcolonial writer, then, is clear: she has opted to remain within history, despite its ravages and cruelties. She has shown in novel after novel her moral disapproval of a stance that refuses to shoulder responsibility for the past and the present and chooses to withdraw from a painful present reality into a romantic or mythicized past [*Cultural Imperialism* 96].

In contrast to Anita Desai, another recent expatriate Indian writer, Amitav Ghosh, presents unusual plots, characters, and incidents that vary from combinations of science fiction and fantasies to tales of Southeast and East Asia in a historical context. Like Desai, Amitav Ghosh began publishing in India and then moved into the world market of English-language fiction, Ghosh is now a resident of New York and teaches at

Columbia University. Born in Calcutta in 1956, Amitav Ghosh spent his early years in Bangladesh (formerly East Pakistan), Sri Lanka, Iran, and India. A graduate of the University of Delhi, Ghosh studied Social Anthropology, receiving a Master of Philosophy and a Ph.D. in 1982 from Oxford University. The fieldwork that he did in Egypt in the village of Lataifa influenced *In an Antique Land* (1992). Amitav Ghosh has also published as a journalist. His fiction includes *The Circle of Reason* (1986), *The Shadow Lines* (1988), *The Calcutta Chromosome* (1996), and *The Glass Palace*, (2000). Ghosh has won several prestigious literary awards in different countries. These include the Prix Medici Etranger, one of France's top literary awards, for *The Circle of Reason*; the prestigious Sahitya Akademi Award in India for *The Shadow Lines*; the Arthur C. Clarke Award in 1997 for *The Calcutta Chromosome*; and the Grand Prize for fiction at the Frankfurt International e-Book Awards in 2001, for *The Glass Palace*. In 1999, Amitav Ghosh won the Pushcart Prize for one of his essays published in the *Kenyon Review*. He lives in Brooklyn with his wife Deborah Baker and their children. His wife is a senior editor at Little, Brown & Co.

Ghosh's first novel, *The Circle of Reason*, is a narrative set in rural India. His second novel, *The Shadow Lines*, deals with the narrator's family in Dhaka and Calcutta and their connections in England. The transition into the New World comes with an unusual novel, *The Calcutta Chromosome* (1996), a work that combines science fiction with the elements of the historical novel. This thoroughly researched, exciting narrative combines the method of the historical novelist with the energy of science fiction and the plot-driven structure of detective novels. The limited character development of *The Calcutta Chromosome* is a characteristic this work appears to inherit from science fiction and the detective novels it uses as models.

The novel's point of view is that of Antar, an Egyptian immigrant who works as a computer programmer and systems analyst for an organization named Life Watch:

> Life Watch was a small but respected non-profit organization that served as a global public health consultancy and epidemiological data bank.... Life Watch had long since been absorbed, along with many other such independent agencies, into the mammoth public health wing of the newly formed International Water Council [*The Calcutta Chromosome* 9].

Antar is an unimportant corporate employee whose first wife dies in pregnancy, plunging him into deep loneliness. The company assigns Antar the task of counseling a maverick epidemiological researcher, Murugan, against undertaking a paid endeavor on the malaria specialist of yesteryear, the late Ronald Ross in Calcutta, India.

The Calcutta Chromosome is a series of episodic narratives related by Murugan to Antar. Most of the novel uses the technique of flashbacks. At the beginning, readers learn that Murugan's ID flashes on Antar's computer screen. With the assistance of a co-worker named Ava, Antar seeks to decode Murugan's mysterious disappearance, which lies at the core of the novel.

Murugan's tale is a wild adventure inclusive of supernatural episodes such as the stories of Phulboni and the phantom stationmaster; of the Bengali journalist Urmila, who joins Murugan in his adventures; of Sonali the movie actress; and of Romen Haldar, who is really the reincarnation of a person from the time of Ronald Ross, an English physician who was awarded the Nobel Prize for discovery of the life cycle of the malaria parasite. The novel contains everyday scenes from the lives of the Indian urban middle class fused with events that have meaning in terms of time traveling, a concept frequently used in science fiction fantasies. Every character that Murugan encounters in India has some connection to a counterpart who lived in the time of Ronald Ross and was in some way linked to his scientific discoveries.

Significant research into both contemporary theories of biology and computer science appears to have been conducted by Ghosh before embarking upon the narrative structure of *The Calcutta Chromosome*. The novel posits the idea of using malaria infection to cure syphilis, a scientific procedure supposedly originated by an Indian woman laboratory worker named Mangala. This discovery by the hypothetical scientist Mangala is called "the Calcutta chromosome":

> if there really is such a thing as the Calcutta chromosome only a person like Mangala, someone who's completely out of the loop, scientifically speaking, would be able to find it.... For what we have here is a biological expression of human traits that is neither inherited from the immediate gene pool nor transmitted into it [*The Calcutta Chromosome* 250].

The novel makes a valuable observation on the politics of contemporary science: "Biologists are under so much pressure to bring their findings into line with politics" (*The Calcutta Chromosome* 251). Mystery, science, thriller, science fiction, the history of tropical medicine are all combined by Ghosh into an extremely absorbing novel.

With *The Glass Palace* (2000), his most recent work, Ghosh creates a very lengthy novel that is similar to the family sagas favored by Vikram

Seth, Anita Desai, and by novelists who continue to compose and publish narratives of epic dimensions in India's regional vernacular languages. Like *The Calcutta Chromosome*, this novel is based upon intensive research. The novel is dedicated to the author's late father, to his war experiences and questioning. Ghosh writes: "In the end my greatest debt is to my father, Lieutenant-Colonel Shailendra Chandra Ghosh. He fought in the Second World War as an officer of the 12th Frontier Force Regiment, a unit of the British Indian Army" (*The Glass Palace* 474).

This novel contains multiple narratives of far away and long ago that are perhaps filled with the expatriate artist's longing for a rich cultural past, as Ghosh states: "In attempting to write about places and times that I knew only at second and third hand, I found myself forced to create a parallel, wholly fictional world.... [E]xcept for King Thebaw, Queen Supayalat and their daughters, none of its principal characters bear any resemblance to real people, living or deceased" (*The Glass Palace* 471)

The family saga in Ghosh's novel was inspired by his research into the history of his own family. Ghosh comments: "The seed of this book was bought to India long before my own lifetime by my father and my uncle, the late Jagat Chandra Datta of Rangoon and Moulmein—'The Prince,' as he was known to his relatives" (*The Glass Palace* 471). However, the transformation of characters and events into a fictional world is complete, as the author comments: "But neither my father nor my uncle would have recognized the crop that I have harvested" (471).

The characters in *The Glass Palace* are from several generations and several branches of the Raha family. The Rahas are Indians who had settled in Burma under British colonial rule. The novel develops the history of three generations from the deposition of King Thebaw to the Japanese invasion of Malaya and Burma during World War II. One branch of the Raha family is represented by the son Dinu, who works in Malaya as a photographer during World War II. Characters of Chinese and Burmese ethnicity play major roles in the stories of the Raha family. The glass palace of the novel's title becomes a dominant metaphor for the many threads of the story woven as a Pan-Asian tapestry of love, friendships, relationships, and marriages between Indian, Burmese, Malaysian, and Chinese people. In the story of Dinu's life in Malaya, there is an actual historical account of the ravages of World War II when the Japanese invaded other Asian nations in Southeast Asia. The scenes in Malaya include the painful end of Saya John. Saya John is a Chinese who relocates from Burma to Malaya only to die a brutal death at the hands of the Japanese in his old age.

The saga of the Raha family in Burma centers around the Indian Rajkumar Raha, a Bengali like the author, orphaned of both his parents by a tropical fever in Mandalay. Rajkumar Raha grows up in Burma and marries Dolly, a Burmese lady-in-waiting to the exiled Queen Supayalat. Rajkumar lives to a ripe age, raising his granddaughter Jaya whose name means victory. Rajkumar's son and daughter-in-law die during World War II in two tragic episodes. Jaya herself is widowed at a young age. She makes a living as a college teacher in India, completing her doctoral dissertation on the history of photography in India. Jaya's son goes to America when he is twenty-two years old, thereby establishing links with the South Asian diasporic experience in the New World.

Jaya also finds a link at an art history conference to her long-lost uncle Dinu, whom she is able to visit in Burma (Myanmar), where he operates the Glass Palace Studio. The recurring allusions to the story of the exiled monarchy contain a careful reconstruction of the palace intrigues of Imperial Burma as well as the military dictatorship of contemporary Myanmar. Amitav Ghosh very carefully protects his sources of information in Myanmar (*The Glass Palace* 473).

The fashionable family saga of South Asian novelists writing for a reading public in South Asia as well as overseas reached mammoth proportions in Vikram Seth's *A Suitable Boy* (1993). The 1,349 pages of Seth's novel really comprise four novels in one. Seth chronicles the lives of four Indian families from the nineteen fifties to the nineteen nineties. *A Suitable Boy* was published in the United Kingdom and the United States, adding international recognition to the recognition he enjoyed in India. The novel reflects Seth's interest in soap operas (Raghavan 1).

Born in 1952 in Calcutta, Vikram Seth grew up in an educated middle-class family. He studied in England at Oxford University, earning a degree in philosophy, politics, and economics. He was enrolled in a Ph.D. program in Economics at Stanford University but did not complete the program. Seth was a Wallace Stegner fellow in Creative Writing at Stanford from 1977 to 1978. From 1980 to 1982, he studied classical Chinese poetry and different languages at Nanjing University in China. Seth published six collections of poetry from 1980 to 1990. His first "novel" was *The Golden Gate* (1986), a transitional narrative work composed in 690 rhyming sonnets, set in San Francisco. Seth entered the realm of traditional fiction with *A Suitable Boy*, which won The Connect Award in 1993. The writing of the novel took almost a decade (Raghavan 2).

Seth acknowledges his debt to nineteenth-century fiction and his downplaying of a strong authorial agenda (Raghavan 3). *A Suitable Boy* chronicles the lives of four upper-middle-class Indian families, three Hindus—the Mehras, the Kapoors, and the Chatterjis—and one Muslim family, the Khans. The novel uses the omniscient third-person effaced narrator in the manner of nineteenth- and early twentieth-century fiction, obviously a conscious choice on the author's part.

Like some of Anita Desai's novels, *A Suitable Boy* begins in the setting of the conflicts between Hindus and Muslims, a problem that has permanently divided South Asia into different countries. The novel's message is in favor of tolerance and peaceful co-existence between different communities. The multiple narrative strands of *A Suitable Boy* chronicle the lives, and often very slow-moving actions, of members of the four different families. The public events of postcolonial India are paralleled by the gradual changes in the lives of characters from generation to generation. These cross-generational changes form the backbone of Seth's novel.

The novel opens with the marriage of Sarita, the older Mehra girl, to Pran Kapoor, and ends with the marriage of the younger Mehra girl, Lata, to Harish. Hence there is a pervasive theme of the search for "a suitable boy." Seth's novel shows how marriages and kinship broaden the reach of the Indian extended family that is in many ways a tyrannical social organization requiring significant conformity from its members. Although there are satiric elements in Seth's characterization, there is significant realism in depicting the lives of the Indian middle class over the last four or five decades of the twentieth century.

By and large, Seth is compassionate in his depiction of individuals caught between their inner selves and their external social world, where behavior is often dictated by hypocrisy and somewhat mercenary social mores. Seth's writing is both tender and funny, like Ved Mehta's portraits of his numerous relatives except that Seth's characterizations are in a fictional format. The richly painted canvas of *A Suitable Boy* is also reminiscent of Anita Desai's theme and character development in that Seth portrays numerous characters leading empty lives in provincial Indian towns.

Somewhat similar to Desai, Mehta, and Seth in its depiction of the hypocrisy and tyranny within the extended family and its oppressive effect on women's lives is Manju Kapur's first novel, *Difficult Daughters* (1998), published by Faber and Faber for distribution worldwide. The author was born in Amritsar, India. She is an English professor at Miranda House College, Delhi University, and the mother of four children. The research for the historical background of this novel took her five years. Kapur's novel has received much praise from reviewers.

Difficult Daughters is basically the life story of one "difficult" daughter of a middle-class Punjabi family in northern India who refuses the traditional arranged marriage in early life and pursues higher education and an independent romantic relationship with one of her professors. The novel begins with the funeral of Virmati, who had chosen to be an organ donor and had requested that her survivors avoid all ceremonies after her cremation. The narrator is Virmati's daughter Ida, who takes the train to

6. Another World, Another Time

Amritsar, where her mother's family still lives. Thus begins Ida's reconstruction of her mother's biography. The novel uses fictional characters and actions but Kapur's method of narration imitates that of biographies that have been carefully researched.

Virmati grew up as the oldest of eleven children, providing continuous help with childcare for her mother, whose life was one of continual childbearing and child raising. Virmati comes under the early influence of her cousin Shakuntala, who has chosen a college education and the career of a science teacher over the traditional arranged marriage. Shakuntala is another "difficult daughter." Set at the time of India's independence movement and the waning of British colonial rule, Kapur's novel emphasizes the quest of women of Virmati's generation for independence and recognition of their individuality. Another such young woman is Swarna Lata, Virmati's roommate in Lahore, who is working on her M.A. and also participates actively in political activities.

The story of Virmati's life is one of struggle against her traditional and somewhat abusive family and the weak character of her lover. The professor who falls in love with Virmati is a married man whose wife was chosen for him when he was a toddler. Both the professor and his wife, who is illiterate, are victims of a tradition that has placed them in an incompatible and loveless marriage to which two children have been born. Virmati turns down the bridegroom chosen for her by her family on the pretext of earning a teaching degree and pursuing a career. The rejected bridegroom is then, ironically, married to the second sister Indumati.

Living away from home in Lahore, Virmati becomes pregnant by Harish, the professor, who continues to visit her. She has an abortion that her liberated friend Swarna Lata helps her arrange. On graduation from the teacher's college, Virmati takes up employment in the princely Sirmaur State at the Pratibha Kanya Vidyalaya, a school for two hundred and fifty girls. She loses this job after Harish comes to visit her and spends the night in her teacher's residence. Bound for the University of Shantiniketan in eastern India, Virmati stops over in Delhi, leading to the intervention of Harish's friend, a poet. This friend insists that Harish marry Virmati, a practice still legal in the nineteen forties till it was banned by the passing of the Hindu Code Bill (Marriage laws for Hindus were set in favor of monogamy through legislation in 1954.)

The novel has a slow exposition that builds up to the rejection of the bridegroom and Virmati's leaving home. Then the talk of her romance and marriage gains momentum with details of her tension-filled life under the same roof with Harish's first wife and his mother, Kishori Devi. A miscarriage and the birth of her daughter Ida are significant events. She works as the principal of an elementary school, and spends several terms away from Harish's home working on her M.A. in Lahore. The Hindu-Muslim communal conflicts give Harish a reason to send his mother, sister, first wife and children back to his hometown.

When Harish relocates to Delhi to head the faculty of a small college, he is able to live with Virmati and Ida. His other children come to live with them for their education but the first wife is permanently separated. Thus, Kapur's novel effectively develops the drama of incompatibility, the economic dependence of wives, the problems of second marriages, which not only existed in South Asian society under the old order but remain social problems today.

Historical research and the creation of dramatic events are central to Vikram Chandra's first novel, *Red Earth and Pouring Rain* (1995). Vikram Chandra, who was born in New Delhi in 1961, has been deeply influenced by his mother, a successful screenplay writer for Indian cinema. In 2000, Chandra served as co-writer for the Bollywood movie *Mission Kashmir*. In 1984, Chandra graduated from Pomona College in California with a B.A. in English, *magna cum laude*. He then attended the Film School at Columbia University in New York. In the library at Columbia University, Chandra found "the autobiography of Colonel James "Sikander" Skinner, a legendary nineteenth-century soldier, half-Indian and half-British" (*www.saja.org* 2). He left school to write the novel *Red Earth and Pouring Rain*, a historical novel of 542 pages that approaches the epic dimensions of Amitav Ghoshi's recent fiction as in *The Glass Palace*.

Carefully researched and developed, like the fiction of Ghosh and Kapur, *Red Earth and Pouring Rain* is written in flowing prose with emphasis upon action in its plot construction and characterization. This novel reached a global audience in 1995 when it was published simultaneously by Penguin in India, Faber and Faber in the U.K., and Little, Brown in the U.S. Reviewers and critics praised Chandra's first novel. Chandra won the David Higham Prize for Fiction and the Commonwealth Writers Prize for Best First Book (*www.saja.org* 1). While working on this novel, Chandra obtained an M.A. at Johns Hopkins University, and an M.F.A. at the University of Houston. He is now resident in Washington, D.C., where he teaches creative writing at George Washington University.

Red Earth and Pouring Rain begins with Abhay, an Indian college student home from America, shooting a white-faced monkey who stole his designer jeans. The family tries to nurse the monkey back to health. The monkey gets hold of their old typewriter and identifies himself as the reincarnation of an eighteenth-century poet named Sanjay. The poet-monkey types out his memories of his past life for his caregiving family. The story is very complicated, with details of battles between European colonial adventurers and the armies of Indian princely states set in the eighteenth century. The narrative includes the palace intrigues of the historical Begum Sumroo, and an actual suicide by fire of a Rajput woman whose European husband has insulted her. It also includes details of interracial relationships and mysterious medicine men, painted on a vast canvas populated with numerous historical and fictional characters. The title comes from an eighteenth-century love song: "But in love/our hearts have mingled/like red earth and pouring rain" (*Red Earth and Pouring Rain* 210).

A parallel tale to that of Skinner in eighteenth-century India is that of the Indian student Abhay who is studying at an American university. Abhay, too, encounters different characters, including his girlfriend Amanda, whose mother posed for a *Playboy* centerfold. Amanda travels with Abhay to India, becomes disappointed and returns to the United States. Sanjay, the monkey narrator, finishes his tale and awaits death according to his contract with Yama, the mythological Hindu god of death:

> Tell the story. But I am done.... Abhay, when I have finished, I shall lay my head in the lap of Yama and I shall listen to your story, and the story will never end, in its maya we will play, and we will find endless delight [*Red Earth and Pouring Rain* 512–572].

There is a clear analogy in this novel to the narrative method of the *Arabian Nights*. The novel's ultimate value is in its richly layered mythopoeic narrative method. Mythopoeia is interwoven with symbolism in Vikram Chandra's *Love and Longing in Bombay* (1997), a collection of long short stories that has received glowing reviews. Two of the stories in the collection were published in *The New Yorker* and the *Paris Review*. The *Paris Review* awarded Chandra the Discovery Prize for the story "Dharma" (www.saja.org 1).

The narrator of *Love and Longing in Bombay* is Subramaniam, who has retired from the civil service. Each story is titled after concepts that have been handed down from ancient Aryan/Hindu culture: "Dharma" (duty or religion), "Shakti" (strength or power), "Kama" (love, lust, desire), "Artha" (wealth, or material goods), and "Shanti" (peace). The stories are set in and around the megalopolis of Bombay (now renamed Mumbai).

In "Dharma" the central character is Jago Antia, a Parsi military officer with an artificial limb who is unable to sell his parents' house. An old servant lives in the house. Antia calls an exorcist and finds out that the property is haunted by the ghost of his older brother, who died as a child. The story recreates Antia's encounter with the ghost in an unusual narrative that encapsulates Antia's joys and nightmares as he remembers that his horseplay as a boy caused his brother to fall to his death:

he saw again Soli backing away, Jehangir reaching up trying to take his hand away from the string ... the solid impact of his small body against Soli's legs ... he's falling with Soli, he feels the impact of the bricks through Soli's body [*Love and Longing in Bombay* 30].

"Shakti" is narrated from the point of view of the maid Ganga, who saves enough money to buy a hovel that she sells to provide a marriage dowry for her daughter. Rival society women Sheila Bijlani and Dolly Boatwalla have to learn to get along because Sheila's son and Dolly's daughter are in love. "Kama" too is about love in that its protagonist, Sartaj Singh, tracks an unsolved homicide, a complicated tale of love and its betrayal between married couples. The investigator Sartaj Singh himself is still in love with his ex-wife Megha, a spoiled and beautiful young woman. "Artha" examines the lives of young people in Bombay, their social lives, local bars, workplaces, and family relationships. The relationships of two homosexual men are included in these Bombay scenes. "Shanti" is similar to "Artha" in its development of the scenes of contemporary life in Bombay.

The first three stories of *Love and Longing in Bombay* are very well-crafted. Vikram Chandra's style contains lively dialogue. He recreates the rhythms of the common man's English that is spoken in India.

With Vikram Chandra, Vikram Seth, Amitav Ghosh, and Anita Desai the reading public of the Americas encounters vast canvases and multi-layered narratives of South Asian life both contemporary and past. The novels and stories offer entry into another world and time through the writers' mastery of the storyteller's art.

7

Narratives of Exile: South Asian Writers in Canada

South Asian fiction writers in Canada may be classified into two groups: one, the first-generation immigrants from South Asia such as Anita Rau Badami and Rohinton Mistry, and two, the Indo-Caribbean migrants such as the late Harold Sonny Ladoo, Neil Bissoondath, and Rabindranath Maharaj. While scholars now tend to emphasize the lack of homogeneity of diasporic South Asian writers, the narratives of South Asian artists in Canada are most commonly narratives of exile, of a long-lost land of the writers' origins. Critic and short-story writer Uma Parameswaran has coined the term SACLIT (South Asian Canadian Literature) to encompass this body of writing. Only the writers more established in terms of scholarly interest are examined closely in this chapter. There are close parallels in SACLIT with the romanticized narratives and fantasies created by recent immigrant writers from South Asia to America. Uma Parameswaran addresses the choices of South Asian Canadian writers in the following terms:

> How can writers dispel the spells of memory and how do we read our diasporic writers? The first question is, of course, should we dispel them? Not entirely, but I believe that both writers and critics of the Indian diaspora need to shift their focus from the original homeland to the present homeland ["Spells of Memory" 10].

Parameswaran also states that "Indo-Canadians, especially of the second wave, romanticize the past, tending to see no evil and brooking no negative views about their native country" (8). But she adds that several well-known writers, such as Rohinton Mistry, Bharati Mukherjee, and Anita Desai, do not belong to the group who romanticize their native culture (8). She compares these satirists to the Indo-Canadian writers of Caribbean origin, "Neil

Bissoondath, the short-lived Harry Sonny Ladoo, and the new writer Rabindranath Maharaj, all of whom tend to have bitter memories, not of the colonial masters but of their native cultures" (8). The tendency to avoid immigrant concerns similar to those that surface in the fiction of Asian American novelists may be linked to Canada's social policy of multiculturalism, which has tended to emphasize the preservation of the "ethnic" in Canada's diverse population groups. In his powerful critique of Canadian multiculturalism, *Selling Illusions* (1994, 2002), Neil Bissoondath, a nephew of V.S. Naipaul, has pointed out that Canada has a long history of intolerance towards immigrants of Asian origin (*Selling Illusions* 30–31). Bissoondath is of the opinion that multiculturalism "has heightened our differences rather than diminished them; it has preached tolerance rather than encouraging acceptance, and it is leading us into a divisiveness so entrenched that we face a future of multiple solitudes with no central notion to bind us" (*Selling Illusions* 197–198). Thus the setting and themes of South Asian fiction writers in Canada remain concerned with either South Asia or with the South Asian communities of the Caribbean.

One of the earliest Indo-Caribbean writers in Canada other than Samuel Selvon was Harold Sonny Ladoo, who was probably born about 1945 in Trinidad. He was a resident of Toronto from 1968, and was tragically murdered during a short visit to Trinidad in the summer of 1973. His short career as a writer was one of hard work and financial struggle. As he worked service jobs to make a living for his wife and son, he was a student at Erindale College. Ladoo received small grants from the Canada Council and the Ontario Arts Council to complete his fiction. *No Pain Like This Body* (1972) acknowledges the Canada Council, and *Yesterdays* (1974) acknowledges both the Canada Council and the Ontario Arts Council. Ladoo's life was that of the proverbial impoverished and struggling artist. His fiction brings to life aspects of life that are both very sad and very funny among the South Asian plantation workers in Ladoo's native Trinidad. Ladoo's portraits are vivid and his recreation of the patois spoken on the plantation dramatic and realistic. While Uma Parameswaran views the fictional world of the Indo-Caribbean artist as negative in some ways, Ladoo's vision of human life on Trinidad's plantation is truly existentialist.

No Pain Like This Body (1972) is an unusual novel. Ladoo's first novel carries a cover and a front-page sketch of an emaciated man. The title and epigraph came from Buddhist scripture, "The Dhammapada":

> There is no fire like passion
> There is no losing throw like hatred;
> There is no pain like this body
> There is no happiness higher than rest.

7. Narratives of Exile

The novel develops an existentialist vision of life among the South Asian agricultural workers of Tola District in Carib Island. There is a map at the beginning of the novel to give readers a sense of place, of location. The story begins with a poor family on a rice plantation where the parents are referred to as Ma and Pa. There are four children: Balraj, who is twelve, Sunaree, ten, and twins Rama and Panday, eight. The father is abusive and feared by the children, who run through the wet and swampy rice fields to keep away from him. When their mother intervenes, he tries to drown her in soapy water in the family's laundry tub. The children live in great poverty with very little clothing and very poor quality food. During the rice-planting month of August, Rama gets a fever with chest pain that the mother tries to treat with home remedies. During a severe storm, scorpions come into their dwelling and bite the children. Eventually the family is able to send Rama and Balraj to the local hospital. Rama is diagnosed with pneumonia and he does not survive. The mother's grief is poignant:

> Ma saw him. "You drink rum and run me chile in dat rain. But it have a God I tell you. I go tell de whole of Tola dat you kill me chile!" [*No Pain Like This Body* 70].

The body is brought home to a wake at which the mother and father blame one another. The mourners get the mother drunk in scenes where the comedy is subsumed by the pathos. The children do not quite understand death. They imagine their dead brother outside the house long after the funeral.

The passing of time in the lives of the agricultural workers is depicted in terms of planting and growing rice. Further tragedy strikes the family when the mother goes mad and disappears. Even the grandparents cannot find her. The novel ends with a storm. The use of children as main characters in this novel heightens the painful conditions of existence on a Trinidad rice plantation that Ladoo recreated possibly from memories of his early life.

If *No Pain Like This Body* emphasizes the tragic, *Yesterdays* (1974) sustains a farcical note throughout. The central character of *Yesterdays* is Choonilal, whose son Poonwa wants to take a Hindu mission to Canada. Poonwa is motivated by his anger against a blonde Christian teacher from Canada who had made his early childhood in school entirely miserable. Choonilal is pressured by his wife Basdai and the community priest. The novel is richly populated with comic characters who tell stories of their past including their sexual exploits. The country store is owned by the homosexual merchant Sook, who has seduced many of the men in the community. Ladoo's daring satiric portrait of a South Asian peasant community in Trinidad ends with an absurd revelation when Rookmin, the wife of Sook, disrobes before the priest to ask if there was any reason in the world for Sook to reject her in favor of sex with men. Gazing lustfully, the priest assures Rookmin that the world has reason. Once again, Ladoo's fiction reaches an existentialist view in suggesting the meaninglessness of human existence.

The career of Ladoo was cut short in 1973, the year Neil Bissoondath arrived in Canada as a young student from Trinidad. Bissoondath received his B.A. in French from York University and taught French and English as a second language. He is currently a full-time writer.

Neil Bissoondath is the son of Sati, the daughter of the Trinidadian journalist and short-story writer Seepersad Naipaul. His maternal uncles are the late Shiva Naipaul, whose literary career ended with his early death at the age forty, and the celebrated V.S. Naipaul. Bissoondath's mother was a teacher of literature, and his early environment influenced his career: "The desire to write came early around the age of nine or ten.... I realized that my mother's brother earned his living by creating these things—books—that I loved. That's when the idea of becoming a writer came to me" (www.nalis.gov.tt.4). Bissoondath has taught at Laval University. His stories often depict the lives of interracial couples like himself and his partner Anne Marcoux, a francophone medical ethics lawyer. Their daughter Elyssa is bilingual. Bissoondath has been an archcritic of Canada's social policy of multiculturalism, and his political-philosophical perspectives are evident in both his fiction and nonfiction. Common themes include the immigrant's confusion and dislocation. An article published in Trinidad states that Bissoondath himself retains very little of his original culture (www.nalis.gov.tt.1). The article also suggests that Bissoondath creates "disillusioned immigrants" who hunger for the island homes they migrated from (www.nalis.gov.tt.1). Bissoondath's first short-story collection, *Digging Up the Mountains* (1986), was much praised. *Worlds Within Her* (1999) was short-listed for the 1999 Governor General's Award in Canada. The novel *A Casual Brutality* (1988) also explores themes of migration, dislocation, and loss. *Selling Illusions* (1994, 2000) carries a powerful political message against Canada's multiculturalism.

Even though *Selling Illusions* is a non-fictional work, it provides insight into Bissoondath's ideas and method as a writer. For instance, diasporic South Asian writers in Canada still continue to write of the lands they left behind. Bissoondath observes repeatedly that Canadian multiculturalism, with its apparent goals of preserving diverse heritages and instilling tolerance, actually prevents the development of a distinctive common Canadian identity among immigrants of diverse groups (223, 224, 239). Bissoondath has also written of the anti-Asian policies and practices in Canadian history. Bissoondath believes of the country of his adoption that

> we are all in the final analysis Canadians, with a common country and common interests.... Children of antagonistic heritages may come to realize that here, in this country, they have more to gain by leaving aside old and perhaps ongoing feuds than by joining in them [*Selling Illusions* 239].

Bissoondath clearly explains that he separates his artistic manifesto from left-wing ideologies. His method originates from creating characters who generate their own compelling narratives: "Characters will emerge unbidden, often arising from stories or events that have etched themselves onto my subconscious, their voices sometimes speaking at the most inconvenient of moments "(Selling Illusions 172).

Bissoondath's short stories in *Digging Up the Mountains* present characters of different ethnic backgrounds who try to cope with displacement, change, oppression, and migration. The emerging vision is almost existentialist, with recurring motifs of alienation and self-division. There are several characters in this collection who are Caribbean immigrants in Canada. Of all the South Asian writers in Canada, Bissoondath has shown some of the problems that immigrants and visitors face in contemporary Canada.

The title of the collection *Digging Up the Mountains* comes from the predicament of Hari Beharry, a wealthy Indo-Caribbean man who must soon flee his homeland because of the ruling government: "Hari looked up. The sun had already sunk behind the mountains: Hari wished he could dig them up too" (*Digging Up the Mountains* 20). Unusual characters emerge: Eugene, the would-be revolutionary from Trinidad; Adrian, the failed immigrant artist from the Caribbean in Toronto, with his sexist statements; the Japanese woman who comes to Canada to study English and returns home, undergoing a process of change and struggle for selfhood where women have traditionally been denied any kind of individuality. She says, "I am a woman, I am a Japanese woman—I still look to the east when I take medicine—and the ties of tradition still bind me.... To understand oneself is insufficient" ("The Cage" 66). The problem of characters coping with life in politically unstable countries is developed in "Insecurity," and the return of a Caribbean immigrant from Canada is developed in "There Are a Lot of Ways to Die."

Bissoondath's characters range from Indo-Caribbean and Afro-Caribbean immigrants in Canada to Hispanic and Japanese characters. Fear of political violence, and the violent revolutions in the Caribbean and Central and South America, are two recurring motifs.

The meaninglessness of both nationalism and political violence is at the core of the ultimate realization of Raj Ramsingh, an immigrant physician from the Caribbean who returns to his homeland of Casaquemada with his wife Jan and their little son Rohan in *A Casual Brutality* (1998). Aja Norgaard comments that Ramsingh's "dream of helping his struggling homeland becomes a nightmare of racial terror and violence, and the defeat of an idealism that could not survive in an environment of hatred, fear, and poverty" (http://aurora.icaap.org/archive/bissoondath.html 2).

Ramsingh's return to Casaquemada is a nostalgic homecoming for him, and an alien experience for his Canadian wife, who keeps hoping that they will return to Canada. The killing of the chicken that is described in detail in the early section of the novel is a presentation of the kind of violence that always underlies the seemingly easygoing style of life of the islands. These premonitions of violent endings are similar to the episodes of political violence and revolutionary uprisings in Bissoondath's short stories. Fanon points out that violence and class conflict are inherent in postcolonial societies (*The Wretched of the Earth* 89, 123).

Ramsingh's connections with the police officer Madera bring out the brutality underlying the island life that Ramsingh has romanticized. Madera advises him to return to where he came from. While Ramsingh knows that the newly independent state of Casaquemada is politically unstable, he lingers on. On the day that his grandfather dies and he is at his grandparents' house, his wife and son are brutally taken out of the house and shot. Bissoondath describes in painful detail, Ramsingh's location of the dead bodies in the police morgue, and the even more painful funeral where the bodies are cremated. The first-person point of view of the novel lends poignancy to Ramsingh's narrative: "And for the first time in what seems an eternity, I realize what I am about—I realize that I am, with my own hands, burning my wife and son. My throat constricts, a gurgling fills my head, my eyes feel filled apart" [*A Casual Brutality* 376].

Like *A Casual Brutality*, Bissoondath's second novel, *The Worlds Within Her* (1999), depicts a Caribbean immigrant married to a Canadian, the death of their child, and the temporary return to the island to scatter her mother's ashes after cremation. The novel uses the point of view of Yasmin, a South Asian from Trinidad who marries an Anglo-Canadian named James Summerhayes in a wedding that the bridegroom's parents choose not to attend because of his mother's racism.

The title emphasizes the complex inner life of the central character Yasmin and the challenges of living. The interracial marriages, the transition from Trinidad to Canada, the sudden death of her young daughter Ariana in an automobile accident, the return to Trinidad to scatter her mother's ashes are all experiences that affect Yasmin's inner world permanently. Listening to the stories of her uncle and aunt in Trinidad on her visit, Yasmin makes discoveries about herself. Finally, she learns that Amie, the housemaid, is her birth mother, not the woman whose ashes she has come to scatter. The novel unravels aspects of Yasmin's past with great skill.

Like Neil Bissoondath, Rabindranath Maharaj writes of the lives of Caribbean immigrants in Canada. Born in Trinidad in 1955, Maharaj worked as a columnist for the *Trinidad Guardian*. He received his M.A. from the University of New Brunswick in 1993 with "The Assault of Strangers" as his project. He has taught high school in Ajax, Ontario. Maharaj has published three collections of short stories: *The Interloper* (1995), *The Writer and His Wife* (1996), and *The Book of Ifs and Buts* (2002). His two novels are *Homer in Flight* (1997) and *The Lagahoo's Apprentice* (2000). Maharaj's autobiography appears in *Death of a Guru* (1977, 1984) formerly published as *Escape into the Light*. Maharaj's writing deals primarily with the experiences of characters from his native Trinidad. Some of the fiction is set in Trinidad, and some of the stories are set in Canada in Caribbean immigrant communities. There are similarities of setting and characterization with Neil Bissoondath's fiction. Like other South Asian writers of immigrant fiction, Maharaj creates antiheroes and losers. The lives of ordinary people make up the core of Maharaj's fictional world. For example, the novel *Homer in Flight* has among its main characters a Trinidadian immigrant who moves from a factory job to become a school librarian.

Maharaj's second collection of short stories, *The Writer and His Wife*, is illustrative of his fictional technique. Maharaj's antiheroes struggle with both heroism and comedy to achieve the limited goals of their daily existence. In "The Librarian" Bashir Ali, the librarian, is a failed romantic who is nevertheless able to bring about necessary improvements in his small-town library. Plain-looking and unsuccessful with women, Bashir Ali is almost a Chekhovian character in a Caribbean setting. "The Writer and His Wife" contains a comedic couple, a big woman with a small husband. Throughout the story the wife maintains that her husband, the writer, is the boss. However, it is only after she dies that the writer is able to publish his writings. The entire story is tinged with irony. "The Metalwork Technician" is Hoobnath Hingoo, who is unhappy at his job and is abusive to his wife till his father-in-law gives him money to open his own machine shop. Many of Maharaj's stories contain static plots with an emphasis on capturing a character experiencing a certain mood, as in "Designs," where the architect Charles Parmassar is somewhat attracted to a woman named Pauline.

Maharaj's autobiography, *Death of a Guru*, stands by itself in that its central motif is that of religious controversy. Born in a Trinidadian Brahmin family, the first-person narrator is placed in training for the hereditary Hindu priesthood. While in training, he is disillusioned by the slack and immoral ways of his teacher and fellow trainees. He writes of his own early bigotry and intolerance toward Christians. He reads Bertrand Russell to find reasons to remain a Hindu and not become a Christian. Then his cousin Krishna, who has become a Christian, takes him to a Christian meeting where he is so deeply moved by the service and hymns that he becomes a Christian. The conversion changes his life, and he persuades other members of his family to become Christians. The autobiographical narrative also links the counterculture of the sixties and seventies to the influence of Hinduism. The narrative concludes with the narrator's participation in missionary activities. In some ways this autobiographical narrative is evocative of Paulo Freire's concept of "cultural invasion" in which a minority's cultural (in this case, religious) values are subsumed by the majority's value system (*Pedagogy of the Oppressed* 133, 134).

At the core of Maharaj's autobiographical writing is the theme of self-discovery and self-awareness. In this aspect Maharaj is similar to Ved Mehta, whose autobiographical writings employ fictional techniques to develop settings and characters. Also like Mehta, the fundamental basis of the autobiographical narrative is one of coming to terms with himself, realizing that his Eastern heritage and Western upbringing are essentially antagonistic.

Anita Rau Badami, who made Canadian best-seller lists with *Tamarind Mem* (1996), is in some ways similar to Maharaj in creating characters from her early life in another country. Badami is an immigrant writer from India who has lived in Canada since 1991. Badami holds a B.A. in English from the University of Madras. She studied journalism at Sophia College in Bombay (Mumbai) and worked for advertising agencies, newspapers, and magazines for seventeen years. She married in 1984 (Mickley 1). Her son was born three years later and she relocated with her family in 1991 to Calgary in Canada (Mickley 1).

Badami's father worked as a mechanical engineer for the Indian Railways (Mickley 1). Settings and characterization in her novel *Tamarind Mem* clearly use many of her autobiographical memories although the novel's main characters are stated to be entirely fictional. *Tamarind Mem* is in two sections: the first-person narrative of the daughter Kamini, followed by the first-person narrative of the mother Saroja, whose sharp tongue earned her the nickname of "tamarind mem" among the domestics in the "railway colonies" (residential communities). Between the two narratives, the reader is able to picture the persistence of colonial social mores in postcolonial India. Saroja and her children live in a large house with two domestic servants. Like *Difficult Daughters*, this novel is also the portrait of a strong-willed mother. Saroja is denied the higher education she desires, and is given in marriage to a man fifteen years her senior. In this clearly loveless marriage of convenience, Saroja raises two daughters while the husband travels on railroad business very frequently. The couple communicates minimally. The husband smokes heavily and dies presumably of cancer. Saroja relocates to an apartment in Madras with her two daughters and adjusts to a more modest income and style of life.

The novel is reminiscent of the gentle and warm narratives of R.K. Narayan, and the fiction of Raja Rao. Various issues emerge, such as English-language education in India that makes it possible for Indians to move from one state to another; the railway colony as its own *polis* with a wide variety of characters who persist in their imitations of colonial behavior long after colonialism has departed. Ingrained in the life depicted by Badami is the persistence of caste and class divisions in Indian society. Also significant is the manner in which Saroja, the mother, is feared for her temper tantrums, and how she gains power in the home over time to eventually browbeat her husband into discarding his pipe and tobacco. Saroja rants and raves:

> "You think you are a bloody English sahib, posing and posturing with that wretched pipe. At least those stupids got their money's worth out of this country before they burnt their lungs out. But you, all can think of is your own pleasure" [*Tamarind Mem* 127].

Her husband reminds her that the British left India twenty-three years ago. Her outburst is symbolically significant because she views her husband (an oppressor in her mind) as the colonial masters of the past, equating his pipe-smoking to the selfishness and greed of the colonial rulers. The juxtaposition in Saroja's mind of power and privilege with colonialist behavior is illustrative of the scars that colonialism has left on the psyches of formerly colonized peoples.

This novel's New World connection emerges in the fact that Kamini, the daughter, is a graduate student in Calgary. From continents away, Kamini tries to understand her mother's unhappy and angry personality and her parents' marriage. Lisa Mickley comments that "Kamini inhabits a different time period from her mother, a fact which makes it difficult for her to fully comprehend her mother's problems at Kamini's present age" (Mickley 4).

Badami's second novel, *The Hero's Walk* (2000), won the Commonwealth Writer's Prize in 2001 for Canada and the Caribbean. Like her earlier novel, *The Hero's Walk* links Canada and India through a child; in this case, the seven-year-old orphan Nandana. Unlike Kamini, who journeys to Canada, Nandana is taken to India by her maternal grandfather Sripathi when her mother, Maya, and her father, Alan Baker, are killed in an automobile crash.

The hero of the title is Sripathi, so named after the "humble" heroes of the Southern Indian classical dance form Bharat Natyam. Sripathi works in an advertising agency and writes letters to editors. He disowns his daughter Maya when she marries a Canadian instead of the Indian suitor chosen by her family for a traditional arranged marriage. Sripathi is a Willy Loman–like character who has spent his whole life in an insignificant job supporting his wife, son, daughter, and unmarried sister. His memories of his early life include his father's unfaithfulness to his mother, and his mother's hypocrisy and domineering ways.

At the center of the plot is Sripathi's journey to Canada, where he arranges for the funeral of his daughter and son-in-law and brings Nandana to live with his family. Little familiar details of Nandana's rebellion in an alien culture and her steady realization that she is in a warm and caring family send the message that human understanding can always overcome cultural differences. The novel is memorable for its recreation of small-town life in Southern India with its joys, sorrows, prejudices, and humor. Nirmal Trivedi aptly comments: "Re-creating and crossing borders, Badami invests herself fully into the lives [of] the Rao household and delivers something much more than a prize-winning novel. She presents us with a case for reflection into the varied domestic sphere from which we all emerge" (Trivedi 2).

Just as Badami is able to recreate the familiar details of life in the ethnic communities where she was raised in India, Indo-Canadian writer Rohinton Mistry creates novels that bring to life characters from the Parsi (Zoroastrian) community to which he belongs. Like the writings of Bapsi Sidhwa, Mistry's novels create unique characters from the Parsi middle class.

Mistry was born in Bombay (Mumbai) in 1952. He holds a B.A. in Mathematics and Economics from the University of Bombay, and a B.A. in English and Philosophy from the University of Toronto. He emigrated to Canada in 1975 (Mitchell 1). Mistry's fiction includes a collection of short stories, *Swimming Lessons and Other Stories from Firozsha Baag* (1987), and the novels *Such a Long Journey* (1991), *A Fine Balance* (1995), and *Family Matters* (2002). He has received several prizes in Canada for his fiction, including the Commonwealth Writer's Prize for his first novel, *Such a Long Journey*. *A Fine Balance* won the Giller Prize, the Royal Society of Literature's Winfried Holtby Prize, and the Los Angeles Award for fiction in 1996 (Mitchell 1). This novel was also short-listed for the Booker Prize.

7. Narratives of Exile

Mistry's short stories, collected in *Swimming Lessons and Other Stories from Firozsha Baag* are set in a fictitious residential community named Firozsha Baag with Parsi characters who confront their inner and outer conflicts in diverse ways. Part of Bombay, Mistry's Firozsha Baag is as full of unusual character types as Manil Suri's apartment building in Bombay in *The Death of Vishnu*. The story "Auspicious Occasion" emphasizes the shabbiness of the apartments in Firozsha Baag where life goes on without change from day to day. The apartment building houses mainly Parsi families and is in very poor condition: "the peeling paint and plaster; in some places the erosion was so bad, red brick lay exposed ... during the monsoon season beads of moisture trickled down the walls, like sweat down a coolie's back, which considerably hastened the crumbling of paint and plaster" ("Auspicious Occasion" 7).

The residents develop friendships and animosities while no one does anything about the crumbling building. The building's resident ghost appears in the narrative of the maid Jacqueline, whom the Parsis call Jaakaylee in a characteristic corruption of words in an unfamiliar language. The "ayah" (maid) compares the Parsis to the British of colonial times, probably in their adoption of Western values, and perhaps in the value they place on light skin color ("The Ghost of Firozsha Baag" 46).

The pranks of the troublesome schoolboy Pesi, who shines a flashlight up girls' miniskirts ("Ghost" 47), the stamp collection of Pesi's father Dr. Mody, the veterinarian, and the brief homosexual involvement of the quiet boy Jehangir ("The Collectors" 98) are all brought to life with realism. Mistry does not idealize life in Bombay's apartments; Dr. Mody's priceless stamp collection has been finally destroyed by insects when his wife gives the albums to Jehangir after his death ("The Collectors" 103).

The women of the community are frequently satirized as being domineering and shrewish in a manner reminiscent of Suri's *The Death of Vishnu*. The strange parade of characters has similarities to Vikram Chandra's characterization in his short stories in *Love and Longing in Bombay*. The title story, "Swimming Lessons," has a first-person narrator resident in Canada who enrolls in an adult swimming program because as a native of Bombay he was never able to take swimming lessons. There is deep irony in this scenario because Bombay is surrounded by the ocean. The narrator describes the predicament of the middle-class Parsi in powerful metaphors:

> The art of swimming had been trapped between the devil and the deep blue sea. The devil was money, always scarce, out of reach; the deep blue sea of Chaupatty beach was grey and murky with garbage, too filthy to swim in ["Swimming Lessons" 234].

The narrator is reminded of how his mother took care of his old and sick grandfather when he observes an old man in his building in Don Mills, Ontario, who is taken care of by his daughter. This concluding story emphasizes the universality of human hardships across continents.

Such a Long Journey is also set in a building in Bombay which houses several Parsi families. The backdrop of the novel is provided by the early-nineteen-seventies regime of the late Prime Minister Indira Gandhi. Mistry shows the Parsi middle class helping the poor class. At the center of the novel is the story of Noble, his wife, son, and daughter, and their daily lives, joys and sorrows. Gustad's friend Jimmy Billimoria dies in a New Delhi prison and receives a mysterious funeral arranged by a Muslim who is not allowed in the Parsis' Tower of Silence (*Such a Long Journey* 323). The reader is not spared the painful realism of vultures devouring dead bodies in these funeral towers.

Unusual characters in the novel include the lame and retarded Tehmul, who is killed when a brick hits him in the head during a protest march (*Such a Long Journey* 333), and Dr. Paymaster, the Parsi physician who supposedly writes formulaic prescriptions for all ailments (*Such a Long Journey* 114). The name "Paymaster" itself is ironically onomatopoeic, for the physician's patients have to keep returning for changes of prescription and repeat payments for office visits.

India in the nineteen seventies is also the backdrop of *A Fine Balance* (1995). The approximate time period of this novel is 1975 in Bombay (Mumbai) during the regime of the late Indira Gandhi, who had declared a State of Emergency in the nation. The novel develops in detail the events of the lives of the poorest classes of society in Bombay in a way somewhat similar to Vikram Chandra and Manil Suri, who also depict the social problems of housing shortages and overcrowding in this megalopolis. Mistry's lively description of life on Bombay's streets among the poor is almost as unforgettable as Victor Hugo's depiction of poverty in nineteenth-century Paris in *The Hunchback of Notre Dame*. Mistry depicts the lives of Bombay's underworld, its untouchables, homeless pavement dwellers, street entertainers such as the Monkey Man, and numerous beggars.

The central character of *A Fine Balance* is Dina Dalal, a Parsi woman who is widowed at a young age when her husband Rustom dies in a hit-and-run accident. Dina begins to make a living as a seamstress in the apartment that her husband had continued to live in after his parents died. The Rent Act that allowed a tenant's family to continue to live in a rented property paying low rents is evoked several times in this novel. Only by the use of criminal violence can property owners regain control of their rental units. Mistry depicts both sides of Bombay's problematic housing situation. The focus of the novel is on Dina Dalal's friendship with the two tailors, Ishvar and Omprakash, whom she hires when her vision begins to weaken in her forties. Dina also takes in a young Parsi student, Maneck Kohlah, as a "paying guest" while he learns the trade of refrigeration and air conditioning. The tailors are of the "untouchable" leather worker caste and have fled their rural communities where their families have been tortured, killed, and burned in their homes in outbreaks of caste/class violence that have remained unpunished by the law.

The predicament of the tailors who are sheltered by Dina when they become homeless and are temporarily incarcerated in Bombay reminds readers of the atrocities committed in India during the nineteen seventies under Indira Gandhi's State of Emergency. The demolition of temporary hutment colonies built by the poor, the jailing of the homeless, the forcible sterilizations of the poor in rural areas, the violent evictions of poor tenants, the underworld criminal activities of the Beggarmaster, whose organization mutilates adults and children to turn them into beggars, create a raw and brutal tale. Mistry does not spare gruesome and sordid details in this grim novel. Once again we are reminded of Fanon's observations in *The Wretched of the Earth* on violence being a by-product of colonization and of class conflict between the postcolonial ruling class and the postcolonial working classes (89, 123).

However, *A Fine Balance* is not without hope as the world of this novel is not devoid of human compassion and friendships. There is a glimmering of hope for the wretched of Bombay in that Dina Dalal, who returns to her brother's home, continues to meet with the tailors even though they have become beggars as a result of caste violence when Ishvar loses his legs and Omprakash is castrated. Maneck Kohlah returns to visit Dina. Maneck works and lives in West Asia but he promises to return again.

If *A Fine Balance* recreates an infernal external world in the gigantic city of Bombay, *Family Matters* (2002) creates the ultimate dysfunctional family in terms of coping with elderly care. *Family Matters* contains an almost existentialist view of Parsi family life, complete with generations of skeletons in the closet such as the mysterious deaths of Nariman Vakeel's wife Yasmin and girlfriend Lucy Braganza, who fall from a rooftop together. Parsi police officers and physicians are handy to provide death certificates and keep out scandal and gossip.

Family Matters pivots on the aging, accident, illness, decline, and eventual death of Nariman Vakeel, a retired English professor in Bombay. The novel's events are set between two Bombay apartments: one in a building called Chateau Felicity, and the other in a building called Pleasant Villa. Nariman Vakeel's life story encapsulates the problems caused by the Parsi religious taboo imposed on marriages outside the faith. Unable to marry his Christian girlfriend Lucy Braganza because of parental objections, Nariman marries Yasmin Contractor, a widow with two children, Jal and Coomy, whom he raises as his own. He has a daughter Roxana with Yasmin. Lucy becomes unbalanced in mind, taking a job as a maid in a downstairs apartment in the building where Nariman lives. Lucy and Yasmin die in a fall from the roof, an incident not explained in the narrative.

During the events of the novel, Nariman is old and ill with Parkinson's disease and osteoporosis. He suffers a leg fracture and his stepchildren Jal and Coomy find it very unpleasant caring for him. They take him to his daughter Roxana's tiny flat in Pleasant Villa. By settling his flat in Chateau Felicity on Coomy and Jal, Nariman has even lost his home.

The slow-moving events of Nariman's period of decline are described in vivid detail including the details of defecation and urination for a bedridden patient. The unpleasant details of bodily functions are described from the point of view of the family members saddled with the responsibility of caring night and day for a bedridden old man who is waiting to die.

The stepdaughter Coomy persuades her brother Jal to damage the plaster of the roof in Nariman's room in Chateau Felicity to declare the apartment unsafe for his return because she does not want to take care of him. She falls victim to her own greed and deceit when she dies in an accident caused by the falling of a beam on her and the incompetent (but inexpensive) Parsi handyman whom she has hired to repair the ceiling.

Upon Coomy's sudden death, Jal improves his relationship with Roxana, her husband Yezad, and their sons. In an act of contrition, he brings old Nariman and his sister's family to live in Chateau Felicity, offering them joint ownership. Roxana's flat in Pleasant Villa is sold when her husband Yezad loses his job managing a sporting goods store. The murder of the store owner Mr. Kapur by criminals with political affiliations once again returns the novel to the chronic violence latent in postcolonial societies.

At the close of the novel, Yezad becomes a religious fanatic, offering serious opposition to his teenaged son, who is dating a non-Parsi girl: I'm warning you, in this there can be no compromise. The rules, the laws of our religion are absolute, this Maharashtrian cannot be your girlfriend" (*Family Matters* 419). As the title itself suggests, this novel offers a series of satiric portraits of Parsi families from one generation to another.

Despite the nostalgia for Old World cultures and bygone ways of living in Third World societies, Rohinton Mistry, like the other Indo-Canadian authors analyzed in this chapter, does not paint rosy pictures of the India he left behind.

Canadian multiculturalism also comes in for questioning when Yezad in *Family Matters* remembers how he was harassed at an interview by a Japanese-Canadian immigration officer when his petition to migrate to Canada was rejected. The rudeness and rejection encountered by Yezad remind us that racism is not the prerogative of any one race, and that there are significant cultural differences between Asians from the Americas and Asians living in Asian countries. Yezad states: "You have sat here abusing us, abusing Indians and India, one of the many countries your government drains of its brainpower, the brainpower that is responsible for your growth and prosperity. Instead of having the grace to thank us, you spew your prejudices and your bigoted ideas. You, whose people suffered racism and xenophobia in Canada, where they were Canadian citizens, put in camps like prisoners of war"... [*Family Matters* 219].

Thus, time and again, South Asian fiction writers in the New World revisit the need for understanding and resolving differences, for comprehending the complex anomalies of the immigrants' style of life, for coming to terms with the deep-seated conflicts of postcolonial societies, and for finally achieving cultural synthesis in the domain of the artist.

8

The Revival of Adolescent Fiction: From Dhan Gopal Mukerji to Mitali Perkins and Indi Rana

Answering questions of canon with regard to a complex and emergent body of literature such as contemporary South Asian fiction published in the Americas is not particularly easy. Selectivity itself implies exclusion, and exclusion can become a problem. Even as this study is composed, new writers of South Asian fiction are beginning their careers, and novels and short stories are appearing in print. The focus on the last half century is primarily an effort to provide the framework of an era for readers of this complex body of fiction in all its variety. Clearly, a variety of models have inspired South Asian writers. Interestingly, most of the literary influences are in the English language—British and American fiction writers. Even though there are allusions to literary works in South Asian languages, the predominant influence is English-language fiction. Undeniably a legacy of the colonial past of Southern Asia, the English language has become a part of the South Asian diaspora's successful ventures amidst New World cultures. This characteristic has influenced the production of literature for children and adolescents by South Asian writers who can look back upon a very strong tradition of vernacular literature for young adults and children in the many different languages of the Indian subcontinent.

South Asian fiction is characterized by psychological verisimilitude in characterization and stylistic sophistication in narrative method. Conflicts in the narrative structure, themes, and characterization are internal rather than external. The writers attempt to move towards resolving differences that arise from conflicts related to the spatial and temporal dimensions of the action. The alienation experienced by the protagonists

8. The Revival of Adolescent Fiction

in the fiction discussed in the preceding chapters is more the anxiety of existence in the postmodern era than the alienation created by exile to a foreign land.

It is interesting to note that South Asian fiction in America begins with adolescent fiction. Many of the problems of identity and self-discovery are present in young adult literature by and about South Asians from the beginning of the twentieth century. The three authors of young adult fiction discussed in this chapter include Dhan Gopal Mukerji, the first South Asian writer in America, Mitali Perkins, a current Asian American author, and diasporic Indian writer Indi Rana, whose novel *The Roller Birds of Rampur* appears on multicultural reading lists for adolescents on three continents. In a sense, these three authors represent the three groups of South Asian writers studied in the preceding chapters—the historical beginners, current Asian American writers of South Asian origin, and diasporic South Asian writers simultaneously published in Asia, Europe, and America.

The beginnings of South Asian adolescent fiction in the United States are well represented in the fiction of the late Dhan Gopal Mukerji. Relegated to neglected corners of libraries, often incorrectly classified among Anglo-Indian fiction writers, Mukerji represents some of the best in Asian American fiction of the early twentieth century. Mukerji's *Gay-Neck: The Story of a Pigeon* (1927) won the prestigious American Newbery Medal in 1928. The work is still recommended on reading lists for American elementary and middle schools.

Mukerji came to the United States from India as a student. He married an American and chose to stay in the U.S., pursuing a career as a writer. Besides *Gay-Neck*, his children's novels include *Kari the Elephant* and *Hari the Jungle Lord*.

Mukerji is an expert at a classical genre of fiction for children and adolescents—the beast fable. Mukerji successfully uses this classical genre which had been revived in the late nineteenth century both in British and American fiction. In *Gay-Neck* he combines the beast fable with autobiographical narratives, giving his tale of the brave tumbler (carrier) pigeon a strong sense of immediacy and adventure.

Mukerji's *Gay-Neck* has similarities to Kipling's *Jungle Book* in bestowing human characteristics upon animals. Gay-Neck's origins, upbringing, and adventures in a family of pet pigeons in Calcutta are described in great detail. The narrative persona is the adolescent boy who owns Gay-Neck. The narrator's discoveries about what is important in the life of a young male parallels Gay-Neck's growth and socialization among other birds.

Gay-Neck was composed during a period when the tale of a boy and his pet was a sure formula for success. One may compare the British writer A.A. Milne's unforgettable Winnie the Pooh, who is owned by a boy named Christopher Robin. Of course Pooh is a teddy bear, not a live animal. There is also the earlier British classic, Beatrix Potter's tale of Peter Rabbit, and the story of the mascot, *The Velveteen Rabbit*, an all-American favorite. The still popular *Charlotte's Web* also belongs to the same literary genre.

Writing for a generation of readers who had access to some highly imaginative adolescent and children's fiction, Mukerji crafted a faraway setting for his readers. He was also able to bring to life the settings in urban Calcutta and in the Himalayan foothills. The breeding and training of pigeons as carriers goes back to ancient and medieval Asian practices. Mukerji's characterization of Gay-Neck (so named from the brightly colored markings on his neck), the pigeon who was recruited by the British Indian Army to serve in World War I as a message carrier, remains unique and unforgettable. Like the author, Gay-Neck travels from India to the West. Unlike the author who chose to stay in America, the "macho" pigeon is injured in the war and returns home to recover.

The central motif of the novel is the experience of fear and the conquest of fear, a very significant theme in describing the development of the male psyche amidst society's expectations of males in traditional roles. There are recurring episodes of the escape of the prey from the predator, a reminder of the daily events of life in nature's world. Gay-Neck's father's death and the gripping episodes of chase by the hawks (Baz) illustrate the terrifying environment that birds face on a daily basis.

When Gay-Neck is recruited for military service, he is shipped with his human trainer Ghond to Armentieres. The narrative point of view shifts periodically from that of the boy to that of the pigeon. In the battlefield, the point of view is that of Gay-Neck himself (because the boy owner is at home in Calcutta). Gay-Neck is hit by shots fired from a plane, and he describes the airplane crash:

> "Then I beheld a strange sight—the airplane had been hit by our men. It swayed, lurched, and fell. But it had done its worst ere it went down in flames—it had hit my right wing and broken it" [Mukerji 161].

Mukerji's sinewy prose brings to life the chases and the battle scenes. The trainer Ghond and Gay-Neck go on a reconnaissance trip all by themselves:

> The place they went to was a forest not far from Ypres, Armentieres and Hazebrouck. If you take a map of France and draw a

line from Calais south almost in a straight line, you will come across a series of places where the British and Indian armies were situated. Near Armentieres there are many graves of Indian Mohammedan soldiers. There are no graves of Indian Hindu soldiers because the Hindus from time immemorial have cremated their dead, and those that are cremated occupy no grave [Mukerji 148].

As colonial subjects, South Asian soldiers have been quite left out of Western historians' accounts of Allied victories in World War I. Mukerji's fiction is a historical reminder of that South Asian presence and the unsung South Asian heroes who gave their lives to the cause of the Allies in World War I.

The overall theme of *Gay-Neck* is peace and love for all beings, especially all races of human beings: "Think and feel love so that you will be able to pour out of yourselves peace and serenity as naturally as a flower gives forth fragrance" (Mukerji 191).

The anxiety of postmodern existence, alienation, and a strong sense of otherness appear very visibly in the South Asian novels that represent strong voices in recent adolescent literature published in America. Alienation and *angst* have, of course, become the hallmarks of contemporary adolescent literature as we know from the immense readership gained by Beverly Cleary's *Dear Mr. Henshaw* and J.K. Rowling's Harry Potter novels.

Mitali Perkins's *The Sunita Experiment* and Indi Rana's *The Roller Birds of Rampur* were both published in the United States in 1993. Both novels have adolescent South Asian girls as protagonists. Both novels continue to occupy places in recommended reading lists on multicultural education for adolescents. Both novels examine adolescent conflicts — boyfriends, peers, parents, seemingly impossible social codes — and intergenerational conflicts, as well as cross-cultural conflicts. Perkins uses the omniscient third-person narrator's point of view, while Rana uses the first person. While Rana's narrative conveys a greater sense of immediacy, Perkins's central character too realizes that most of the conflicts — cross-cultural and intergenerational — are those that she experiences from her own perception of situations and other people.

Indi Rana's *The Roller Birds of Rampur* begins with her purpose of exploring cross-cultural conflicts among diasporic South Asian adolescents. A resident of India, Rana writes that the book grew out of her own experiences of growing up in England, the U.S., and Canada as well as the experiences of her nieces and nephews (Rana v). Rana's novel contains the story of Sheila Mehta, a South Asian adolescent in an English high school who literally has to visit her grandparents in India in order to reconcile herself to the cultural conflicts in her life. It all begins with the English boyfriend Jimmy. Sheila states, "I didn't think about what our families might think,... I didn't realize how unusual it was for an English boy to be going with an Indian girl" (Rana 5). Sheila has always felt herself to be British. She reflects:

> But Dad and Mum never played the heavy Indian parents with Rachna and I, not like my friend Sunaina's parents did. They never drummed into our heads our Indian-ness, our traditions, the dangers of going out with boys, the way they did in England; Mum and Dad were a little unusual [Rana 5].

The reality of her non-English origins is brought home to her by her odd reception by Jimmy's mother who says in shock at Sheila's race: "Sheila? Oh! But...I thought Sheila was an English name!" (12). The maternal disapproval ends the year-long romance: "He started to avoid me at school, then. Stopped calling. And the silences grew, reliably, solidly, dependably" (13).

Jimmy's rejection of Sheila bonds the protagonist more closely with her friend Sunny, who works in her parents' South Asian grocery store after high school. Sunny, or Sunaina, Singh has been raised to wear traditional Indian clothes, and she does not aspire to attend college. She is going to be "married off" in an arranged marriage.

Coping with rejection, Sheila travels to New Delhi hoping to attend university there. In New Delhi, her annoying cousin Tinkoo asks her why she wants to study in India as college students in New Delhi are mostly interested in study-abroad programs to broaden their horizons of opportunity. Sheila also discovers that she cannot quite fit into the social rounds and chit-chat of her relatives in New Delhi. Traveling to her grandparents' rural estate in Rampur in the central part of India, Sheila is confronted by aspects of rural Indian culture that she cannot quite comprehend. Her cousin Bumpy explains to her that there are "two Indias: India of the cities, two hundred million Westernized consumers, and the India of the country, Bharat, which is all the rest" (259).

Despite feeble protests, Sheila is cajoled into wearing the salwar-kameez, or traditional Indian pantsuit, by her grandmother. In her British dresses, she looks too much like an Indian movie heroine to be free of lustful males gazing at her in Rampur. Her grandmother explains: "The good women are modest and decorous in their dress" (114).

Sheila takes a dislike to the mores of rural Indian society:

> What was *wrong* with these boys? Couldn't they behave normally

with girls? Weren't we also people? Did the fact of my having a female body have to make such a difference? School in London, I thought, was *healthy* compared to this! ... Here, bodies came first and got in the way of people being people [130].

She is also disconcerted to find that her North London accent gives her a comical air among her Indian relatives to whose ears her speech sounds like an outdated relic of colonial times (131).

At the climax of the novel, Sheila and her childhood acquaintance Munnia are at a village festival when there is an attack by a bandit gang led by a woman. Munnia's husband Ram Prasad dies in the bandit attack. Munnia's grief leaves Sheila totally confused about the meaning of life and death in the land of her heritage that she has come to explore and comprehend:

> Then I began to see my life was even more complicated than I'd thought. I had to get to grips with four parallel problems. I was a female; I was educated and I would go *on* being as educated as my brain could handle; I was Indian living in England; *and* I had no traditions that told me what to do. I think I've never felt as desperate as I did that moment when I said, "Munnia," and couldn't go on [152–153].

Sheila's grandfather tries to explain the meaning of the Hindu concept of "dharma" or "right behavior" (156) to her. However, she remains upset and rebellious when the priest arrives to offer spiritual comfort to Munnia: "Karma? Is that all you can say? Her husband's been killed, and all you can say is it's her karma?" (186).

Interestingly, just as Sheila could not accept her negative experience with inter-racial dating in England, she cannot accept the fatalism of rural India. "Fate! Destiny! Fatalism! Karma! I *couldn't*, I *wouldn't* accept it!" (188)

Sheila's grandfather patiently explains the cause-and-effect relationships in Hindu philosophy and its meaning of life and death (209). Sheila achieves some degree of resolution of the conflicts she experiences as she learns the name of a bird she admires: "It's a big bird with lovely turquoise and ultramarine on its wings. It's got sort of browny gray on the top" (214). This bird, she learns, is the "roller bird." The bird to her is a symbol of India:

> "That's a neelkanth, a roller bird," Grandpa said promptly.
>   "Lovely, isn't it?"
>   "Roller bird?" I said, trying out the name [214].

Watching the roller birds, Sheila finds it possible to reconcile her Indian origins and her British upbringing:

> And I remembered, suddenly, where I'd heard something like, "I am what I am." It's the Bible. It's what God said to Moses on the mountain, when he revealed his ten commandments. "I am that I am" [294].

Sheila's experiences in India constitute an adolescent's rite of passage into adulthood. Sheila achieves both self-definition and self-discovery. The novel's conclusion finds an adult Sheila who is attending a university in England:

> Living in England is my karma, and that it's really okay is a little bit of dharma.... when I got hauled up by the statistics professor in front of the whole class for daydreaming, well, I took that with a pinch of dharma, too! [295]

Mitali Perkins is an Asian American teacher and author who has a Web site for young immigrants where she posts the following:

> A part of you rises above the steamy confusion of diversity to glimpse the common and universal. You recognize the ache that makes us all feel like strangers, even in the middle of comfortable homogeneity. You understand the soul's craving for a real home because yours is never sated with a counterfeit version (*www.mitaliperkins.com/frcontents.htm* 1).

Although *The Sunita Experiment* is the most acclaimed of her works, Perkins has also authored *Monsoon Summer*, *The Bamboo People*, *Lost Hills*, and *Rickshaw Boy*. Born in Calcutta (now renamed Kolkata) as one of the three daughters of an engineer, Perkins grew up as a diasporic South Asian. In her infancy, the family moved to Ghana, then to Cameroon, Mexico, London, and New York City, finally settling in the San Francisco Bay Area suburb of Martinez, when the author was in seventh grade (*www.mitaliperkins.com/aboutme.htm* 1). Raised in an immigrant Hindu family, she is married to a Presbyterian minister and has twin sons. She is a resident of Massachusetts. Perkins states that she began writing at about age ten and that she is deeply influenced by classic American children's literature such as the work of "Laura Ingalls Wilder, L.M. Montgomery, L.M. Alcott, Frances Burnett, Elizabeth Enright, Sidney Taylor, L.M. Weber" (*www.mitaliperkins.com/aboutme.htm* 1). Coming to America in middle school herself, Perkins has recreated the characteristic dilemmas of middle school students in such works as *The Sunita Experiment*.

Unlike Indi Rana's Sheila, the protagonist of Mitali Perkins's *The Sunita Experiment* is in middle school. Sunita does not visit her grandparents; instead, her grandparents visit her family in the United States. Resentful of her grandparents' visit, and the new rule of "no boys" at her home, Sunita's little romance with her European-American classmate Michael almost comes to an end. But unlike Sheila's racist boyfriend Jimmy, Michael is a liberal knight-in-shining-armor who favors cultural diversity and assimilation. This novel is set in a California suburb.

When thirteen-year-old Sunita's maternal grandparents arrive from India for a year-long visit, her mother takes leave from her job as a college chemistry instructor to take care of her parents. The family's average American household routines are replaced by Indian-style household routines and rules that the adolescent Sunita resents quite openly:

> She was mad at Mom for being so wishy-washy, but at the same time she was secretly relieved. Her grandmother and grandfather were so...different. And Michael was so...well, so *normal* [14].

Most of Sunita's efforts in school are concentrated upon fitting in with her friends. And even without the new rule of "no boys" visiting her house, Sunita would not invite Michael Morrison (a popular boy who plays tennis very well) to her house to meet her foreign grandparents.

Sunita's adolescent crush on the middle school athlete causes her a great deal of emotional turmoil when she finds LeAnn, a cheerleader whom she dislikes, getting quite close to Michael. Sunita complains to her friend Liz about her "weird family" (86). Liz responds with "I love your family, Sunita Sen" (86). But Liz's acceptance does not matter to Sunita because Liz is not part of the school's most popular crowd of teenagers.

Imagining that she has lost Michael's friendship to LeAnn, Sunita leaves a tennis game early. When Michael telephones to inquire why she left early, Sunita is compelled to confront her own inner conflicts on cross-cultural matters, and she states that Michael and LeAnn are after all very much alike before she hangs up on him. The barrier that Sunita builds between herself and her friends at school allows her some time to reflect upon her own place in two groups—her peers at school, and her family. She realizes that she is an individual in her own right, quite different from both groups. She also realizes that she is accepted by both groups for her positive personal characteristics. Liz tells her that she is "cute and smart and fun to be with" (86). However, the demons of cross-cultural and intergenerational differences are still not quite dead, and as the novel's action proceeds towards resolution, Sunita has to wrestle these demons to the ground, quite literally.

As she spends less time with friends from school, Sunita helps her grandfather, whom she calls "Dadu," in the garden. Dadu becomes her ally in coping with the imposition of Indian-style domestic rules by her grandmother "Didu." From Dadu, she also learns about her Indian heritage. With Dadu's intervention, Didu understands why their daughter, Sunita's mother, needs to go back to her job because she really misses teaching chemistry (155).

And it is also in defense of her grandfather, who is being ridiculed in the mall by a group of intolerant schoolmates, that Sunita learns to speak up for her very traditional South Asian grandparents instead of being ashamed of them:

> Sunita stared at LeAnn for a few seconds. "That happens to be my grandfather, LeAnn Schaeffer," she said. "And he has more class in his little finger than you'll ever have in your entire life. I feel sorry for *you*" [168].

The vanquished LeAnn is reduced to tears while Dadu takes Sunita and Liz to an ice-cream parlor (168). They are joined by Michael Morrison, who explains his real attitude towards LeAnn, as well as intergenerational differences of opinion on cross-cultural understanding:

> "Did LeAnn send you over here as her defense lawyer or something?"
> Michael took a deep breath, as though he was trying to hold his patience. "No, Sunni, she didn't," he said slowly. "But I try to defend her when I can. We grew up together, you know, and she's kind of like a sister" [169].

With Michael and Dadu as her allies, Sunita is able to send her mother back to work, and get rid of the "no boys" rule. The novel's ending celebrates cross-cultural understanding among the new generation of American middle schoolers who attend a party at Sunita's house where her grandparents too enjoy interacting with her friends.

While Sunita's process of self-discovery is much less painful than that of Sheila in *The Roller Birds of Rampur*, both adolescent protagonists undergo rites of passage in which they realize that they are first human beings and individuals before they decide to conform to the rules of any particular cultural group at a given place or time. It is this recognition of difference, and of the need to resolve differences, that remains the recurring motif of South Asian fiction in the last half century. The lasting educational significance of these works of adolescent literature is that they evoke the concept of "cultural synthesis" developed by Paulo Freire:

Those who are invaded, whatever their level, rarely go beyond the models which the invaders prescribe for them. In cultural synthesis there are no invaders, hence there are no imposed models. In their stead, there are actors who critically analyze reality (never separating this analysis from action) and intervene as subjects in the historical process [*Pedagogy of the Oppressed* 162].

Works Cited

Chapter One

Barthes, Roland. *Critical Essays*. Trans. Richard Howard. Evanston, Ill.: Northwestern University Press, 1972.
_____. *Image, Music, Text*. Trans. Stephen Heath. New York: Hill and Wang, 1977.
Bhabha, Homi K. *Cambridge History of Literary Criticism Vol. 8: From Formalism to Poststructuralism*. Cambridge: Cambridge University Press, 1995
_____. *The Location of Culture*. New York: Routledge, 1994.
Chhaya, Mayank. "Short, Succinct and Savory." *http://www.literateworld.com/english/2002/bookshelf/july/bjul21.html*, July 21, 2002.
Derrida, Jacques. *Of Grammatology*. Trans. Gayatri Chakravorty Spivak. Baltimore: The Johns Hopkins University Press, 1976.
Dowell, William, et al. "The Golden Diaspora." *Time*, June 19, 2000: B28.
Fanon, Frantz. *The Wretched of the Earth*. New York: Grove, 1963.
Freire, Paulo. *The Pedagogy of the Oppressed*. New York: Continuum, 1993 (First published 1970).
Kanaganayakam, Chelva. *Counterrealism and Indo-Anglian Fiction*. Waterloo, Ont.: Wilfrid Laurier University Press, 2002.
Kreisler, Harry. "Conversation with Author and Diplomat Shashi Tharoor." *Conversations with History*, Institute of International Studies, University of California, Berkeley: 1-5. *http://globetrotter.berkeley.edu/people/Tharoor/html*, Jan. 3, 2001.
Lessinger, Johanna. *From the Ganges to the Hudson: Indian Immigrants in New York City*. Boston: Allyn and Bacon, 1995.
Lichtenstein, David P. "A Brief Biography of V.S. Naipaul." Caribbean Web. *www.postcolonial.org/caribbean/naipau l/bio./html*, July 26, 2000.
Lim, Shirley Geok-lin, ed. *Asian-American Literature*. Lincolnwood, Ill.: NTC, 2000.
Naipaul, V.S. "One But of Many." *In a Free State*. London: Andre Deutsch, 1971.
_____. "Two Worlds." Nobel lecture, Dec. 7, 2001. *www.nobel.se/literaturelaureates/2001/naipaul.lecture*.

Ramchand, Kenneth. *The West Indian Novel and Its Background*. New York: Barnes & Noble, 1970.
Salick, Roydon. *The Novels of Samuel Selvon: A Critical Study*. Westport, Conn.: Greenwood, 2001.
Singer, Isaac Bashevis. Nobel lecture. Dec. 8, 1978. *www.nobel.se/literaturelaureates/1978/singer.lecture*.
Singh, Rashna. *The Imperishable Empire: A Study of British Fiction in India*. Washington, D.C.: Three Continents Press, 1988.
Sonnenberg, Ben. "Tambimuttu in New York." *Bookend* in *The New York Times*, Sept. 21, 1997: 1–4. *www.nytimes.com/books/97/09/21/bookend/bookend.html*, January 5, 2002.
"UK writer Naipaul wins Nobel award." Oct. 11, 2001. cnn.com/SPECIALS/2001/nobel, January 4, 2002.
Wallia, C.J.S. "Dhan Gopal Mukerji's *Caste and Outcast*." *IndiaStar Review of Books*, *http://www.indiastar.com/wallia31.htm*, August 9, 2003.
Zaman, Niaz. *A Divided Legacy: The Partition in Selected Novels of India, Pakistan, and Bangladesh*. Dhaka: The University Press Limited, 1999.

Chapter Two

Barratt, Harold. "Sam Selvon's Tiger: In Search of Self-Awareness." *Reworlding: The Literature of the Indian Diaspora*, E.S. Nelson, ed. New York: Greenwood, 1992.
Feder, Lillian. *Naipaul's Truth: The Making of a Writer*. New York: Rowman and Littlefield, 2001.
Hayward, Helen. *The Enigma of V.S. Naipaul: Sources and Contexts*. New York: Palgrave Macmillan, 2002.
Lichtenstein, David P. "A Brief Biography of V.S. Naipaul." Caribbean Web, *www.postcolonial.org/caribbean/naipaul/ bio.html*, July 26, 2000.
Naipaul, V.S. *The Enigma of Arrival*. New York: Alfred Knopf, 1987.
_____. *A House for Mr. Biswas*. London: Andre Deutsch, 1961.
_____. *In a Free State*. London: Andre Deutsch, 1971.
_____. *The Suffrage of Elvira*. London: Andre Deutsch, 1958.
Ramraj, Victor. "Still Arriving: The Assimilationist Indo-Caribbean Experience of Marginality." *Reworlding: The Literature of the Indian Diaspora*, E.S. Nelson, ed. New York: Greenwood, 1992.
Salick, Roydon. *The Novels of Samuel Selvon: A Critical Study*. Westport, Conn.: Greenwood, 2001.
Selvon, Samuel. *Turn Again Tiger*. London: MacGibbon & Kee, 1958.
"A song of lost islands." *The Economist*, Dec. 10, 1994: 93.

Chapter Three

Bhabha, Homi K. *The Location of Culture*. New York: Routledge, 1994.

Caute, David. "Mehta." *Contemporary Literary Criticism*. Vol. 37. Detroit: Gale, 1986.
Crane, Ralph J. *Ruth Prawer Jhabvala*. New York: Twayne, 1992.
Gordon, Leonard A. "Mehta." *Contemporary Literary Criticism*. Vol. 37. Detroit: Gale, 1986.
Hardgrave, Robert L. Jr. "Mehta." *Contemporary Literary Criticism*. Vol. 37. Detroit: Gale, 1986.
Jablons, Pam. "Mehta." *Contemporary Literary Criticism*. Vol. 37. Detroit: Gale, 1986.
Jhabvala, Ruth Prawer. *Heat and Dust*. New York: Harper & Row, 1975.
_____. "How I Became a Holy Mother." *Out of India: Selected Stories*. New York: William Morrow, 1986.
_____. "The Interview." *Out of India: Selected Stories*. New York: William Morrow, 1986.
_____. "Passion." *Out of India: Selected Stories*. New York: William Morrow, 1986.
_____. "Two More Under the Indian Sun." *Out of India: Selected Stories*. New York: William Morrow, 1986.
Johnson, Gerald W. "Mehta." *Contemporary Literary Criticism*. Vol. 37. Detroit: Gale, 1986.
Jones, Mervyn. "Mehta." *Contemporary Literary Criticism*. Vol. 37. Detroit: Gale, 1986.
Kenny, Anthony. "Mehta." *Contemporary Literary Criticism*. Vol. 37. Detroit: Gale, 1986.
Matthews, Herbert L. "Mehta." *Contemporary Literary Criticism*. Vol. 37. Detroit: Gale, 1986.
Mehta, Ved. *Continents of Exile: All for Love*. New York: Thunder's Mouth Nation Books, 2001.
_____. *Face to Face*. Boston: Little, Brown, 1957.
_____. *The Ledge Between the Streams*. New York: W.W. Norton, 1984.
_____. *Mamaji*. New York: Oxford University Press, 1979.
_____. *Sound-Shadows of the New World*. New York: W.W. Norton, 1985.
_____. *The Stolen Light*. New York: W.W. Norton, 1989.
_____. *Vedi*. New York: Oxford University Press, 1982.
Nossiter, Bernard. "Mehta." *Contemporary Literary Criticism*. Vol. 37. Detroit: Gale, 1986.
Scott, Paul. "Mehta." *Contemporary Literary Criticism*. Vol. 37. Detroit: Gale, 1986.
Sucher, Laurie. *The Fiction of Ruth Prawer Jhabvala: The Politics of Passion*. New York: St. Martin's, 1989.
Wain, John. "Mehta." *Contemporary Literary Criticism*. Vol. 37. Detroit: Gale, 1986.
Zaman, Niaz. *A Divided Legacy: The Partition in Selected Novels of India, Pakistan, and Bangladesh*. Dhaka: The University Press, 1999.

Chapter Four

Alam, Fakrul. *Bharati Mukherjee*. New York: Twayne, 1996.

Works Cited

Carb, Alison B. "An Interview with Bharati Mukherjee." *The Massachusetts Review*, 29.4 (1988): 645–654.

Chua, C.L. "Passages from India: Migrating to America in the Fiction of V.S. Naipaul and Bharati Mukherjee." *Reworlding: The Literature of the Indian Diaspora*, E. S. Nelson, ed. Westport, Conn.: Greenwood, 1992.

Desai, Mahadev. "Books: Stories of Second Chances." *Khabar Magazine*, July 2001: 38.

Divakaruni, Chitra Banerjee. *Arranged Marriage*. New York: Anchor Books, 1995.

_____. *The Mistress of Spices*. New York: Anchor Books, 1997.

_____. *Sister of My Heart*. New York: Doubleday, 1999.

_____. *The Unknown Errors of Our Lives*. New York: Doubleday, 2001.

_____. *The Vine of Desire*. New York: Doubleday, 2002.

Frye, Northrop. *Anatomy of Criticism: Four Essays*. Princeton: Princeton University Press, 1959.

Grewal, Gurleen. "Born Again American: The Immigrant Consciousness in Jasmine." *Bharati Mukherjee: Critical Perspectives*, E.S. Wilson, ed. New York: Garland, 1993.

Mukherjee, Bharati. *Darkness*. Markham, Ont.: Penguin, 1985.

_____. *Desirable Daughters*. New York: Hyperion, 2002.

_____. *The Holder of the World*. New York: Knopf, 1993.

_____. *Jasmine*. New York: Grove, 1989.

_____. *Leave It to Me*. New York: Ballantine, 1997.

_____. *The Middleman and Other Stories*. New York: Grove, 1988.

Nelson, Emmanuel S. "Introduction." *Bharati Mukherjee: Critical Perspectives*, E. S. Nelson, ed. New York: Garland, 1993.

Pati (Wong), Mitali. "Love and the Indian Immigrant in Bharati Mukherjee's *Short Fiction*." *Bharati Mukherjee: Critical Perspectives*, E. S. Nelson, ed. New York: Garland, 1993.

Powers, Janet M. "Sociopolitical Critique as Indices and Narrative Codes in Bharati Mukherjee's *Wife* and *Jasmine*." *Bharati Mukherjee: Critical Perspectives*, E. S. Nelson, ed. New York: Garland, 1993.

Sharma, Maya Manju. "The Inner World of Bharati Mukherjee: From Expatriate to Immigrant." *Bharati Mukherjee: Critical Perspectives*, ed. E.S. Nelson, ed. New York: Garland, 1993.

Stone, Carole. "The Short Fictions of Bernard Malamud and Bharati Mukherjee." *Bharati Mukherjee: Critical Perspectives*, E. S. Nelson, ed. New York: Garland, 1993.

Upadhyay, Samrat. "Arranged Marriage: Between Third World and First." *Review of Books*, Oct. 26, 1997, *The Kathmandu Post. www.south-asia.com/Ktmpost/1997/Oct/Oct26-ed.html*: 2–4.

Wong, Eugene F. *On Visual Media Racism: Asians in American Motion Pictures*. New York: Arno, 1978.

Woolf, Virginia. "A Room of One's Own." *The Norton Anthology of English Literature*. 7th edition. New York: Norton, 2001.

Chapter Five

Hogan, Ron. "Akhil Sharma." *Beatrice Interviews.* www.beatrice.com/interview/sharma/2000: 1.
Lahiri, Jhumpa. "Contributors' Notes." The *Best American Short Stories 2000*, Katrina Kenison, ed. New York: Houghton Mifflin, 2000.
_____. "The Interpreter of Maladies." *Interpreter of Maladies: Stories.* New York: Houghton Mifflin, 1999.
_____. "Mrs. Sen's." *Interpreter of Maladies: Stories.* New York: Houghton Mifflin, 1999.
_____."A Temporary Matter." *Interpreter of Maladies: Stories.* New York: Houghton Mifflin, 1999.
_____. "The Third and Final Continent." *Interpreter of Maladies: Stories.* New York: Houghton Mifflin, 1999.
_____. "This Blessed House." *Interpreter of Maladies: Stories.* New York: Houghton Mifflin, 1999.
An Obedient Father. New York: Farrar, Strauss & Giroux, 2000.
Reeder, Allan. "A Conversation with Akhil Sharma." *The Atlantic Monthly,* Jan. 1997. *www.theatlantic.com/unbound/factfict/asharma.htm.*
Sharma, Akhil. "Cosmopolitan." *The Best American Short Stories 1998*, Garrison Keillor with Katrina Kenison, eds. New York: Houghton Mifflin, 1998.
Sidhwa, Bapsi. *An American Brat.* Minneapolis: Milkweed, 1993.
_____. *The Bride.* New York: St. Martin's, 1983.
_____. *Cracking India.* Minneapolis: Milkweed, 1991.
Suri, Manil. *The Death of Vishnu.* New York: HarperCollins, 2001.
Upadhyay, Samrat. "The Good Shopkeeper." *The Best American Short Stories 1999.* Amy Tan with Katrina Kenison, eds. New York: Houghton Mifflin, 1999.
Zaman, Niaz. *A Divided Legacy: The Partition in Selected Novels of India, Pakistan, and Bangladesh.* Dhaka: The University Press Ltd., 1999.

Chapter Six

Afzal-Khan, Fawzia. *Cultural Imperialism and the Indo-English Novel.* University Park: The Pennsylvania State University Press, 1993.
Chandra, Vikram. *Love and Longing in Bombay.* New York: Little, Brown, 1997.
_____. *Red Earth and Pouring Rain.* New York: Little, Brown, 1995.
Desai, Anita. *Clear Light of Day.* London: Heinemann, 1980.
_____. *Fasting, Feasting.* New York: Houghton Mifflin, 1999.
Ghosh, Amitav. *The Calcutta Chromosome.* New York: Avon, 1995.
_____. *The Glass Palace.* New York: Random House, 2001.
Julik, Rebecca. "Anita Desai." *Voices from the Gaps: Women Writers of Color.* Feb. 28, 1999, *http://voices.cla.umn.edu/authors/AnitaDesai.html*, Dec. 24, 2002.
Kanaganayakam, Chelva. *Counterrealism and Indo-Anglian Fiction.* Waterloo, Ont.: Wilfrid Laurier University Press, 2002.

Kapur, Manju. *Difficult Daughters*. London: Faber and Faber, 1998.
Raghavan, Amit. "Vikram Seth." Spring 1999. *http://www.emory.edu/ENGLISH/Bahri/Seth.html*, Dec. 24, 2002.
Seth, Vikram. *A Suitable Boy*. New York: HarperCollins, 1993.
South Asian Journalists Association. "Vikram Chandra." Jan. 28, 1998, *http://www.saja.org/chandra.html*, Dec. 24, 2002.

Chapter Seven

Badami, Anita Rau. *The Hero's Walk*. New York: Ballantine Books, 2000.
_____. *Tamarind Mem*. Toronto: Penguin, 1998.
Bissoondath, Neil. *A Casual Brutality*. New York: Penguin, 1989.
_____. *Digging Up the Mountains*. New York: Penguin, 1986.
_____. *Selling Illusions: The Cult of Multiculturalism in Canada*. Toronto: Penguin, 2002.
_____. *The Worlds Within Her*. London: William Heinemann, 1999.
Fanon, Frantz. *The Wretched of the Earth*. New York: Grove, 1963.
Freire, Paulo. *The Pedagogy of the Oppressed*. New York: Continuum, 1993 (first published 1970).
Ladoo, Harold Sonny. *No Pain Like This Body*. Toronto: Anansi, 1972.
_____. *Yesterdays*. Toronto: Anansi, 1974.
Maharaj, Rabindranath. *The Death of A Guru* (with Dave Hunt). Eugene, Ore.: Harvest House, 1984.
_____. *The Writer and His Wife and Other Stories*. Leeds, Yorkshire: Peepal Tree, 1996.
Mickley, Lisa. "Anita Rau Badami." Spring 1998. *http://www.emory.edu/ENGLISH/Bahri/Badami.html*, June 27, 2002.
Mistry, Rohinton. *Family Matters*. New York: Alfred A. Knopf, 2002.
_____. *A Fine Balance*. New York: Vintage Books, 1996.
_____. *Such a Long Journey*. New York: Vintage Books, 1992.
_____. *Swimming Lessons and other Stories from Firozsha Baag*. New York: Vintage Books, 1997.
Mitchell, Tom. "Rohinton Mistry." Fall 2000. *http://www.emory.edu/ENGLISH/Bahri/Mistry.html*, December 24, 2002.
Norgaard, Aja. "Up and Coming" (interview). Fall 1989. *http://aurora.icaap.org/archive/bissondath.html*, June 8, 2003.
Parameswaran, Uma. "Dispelling the Spells of Memory: Another Approach to Reading our Yesterdays." *2000 Proceedings of the Red River Conference on World Literature*. Vol 2. *http://www.ndsu.edu/RRCWL/V2/uma.html*, November 7, 2003.
Sunday Guardian. Feb. 25, 2001. *www.nalis.gov.tt/Biography/NeilBissoondath.htm*, June 8, 2003.
Trivedi, Nirmal. Review of *The Hero's Walk*. *http://www.popmatters.com/books/reviews/heros-walk.html*, July 3, 2003.

Chapter Eight

Freire, Paulo. *The Pedagogy of the Oppressed*. New York: Continuum, 1993 (first published 1970).
Mukherji, Dhan Gopal. *Gay-Neck: The Story of a Pigeon*. New York: Dutton Children's Books, 1927.
Perkins, Mitali. "An Interview with Myself." *http://www.mitaliperkins.com/aboutme.htm*, August 10, 2003.
_____. *The Sunita Experiment*. Boston: Little Brown, 1993.
_____. "What's on Indian-American Author Mitali Perkins' Fire Escape." *http://www.mitaliperkins.com/fircontents.htm*. August 9, 2003.
Rana, Indi. *The Roller Birds of Rampur*. New York: Henry Holt, 1993.

Bibliography

Afzal-Khan, Fawzia. *Cultural Imperialism and the Indo-English Novel*. University Park: The Pennsylvania State University Press, 1993.
Alam, Fakrul. *Bharati Mukherjee*. New York: Twayne, 1996.
Badami, Anita Rau. *The Hero's Walk*. New York: Ballantine, 2000.
_____. *Tamarind Mem*. Toronto: Penguin, 1998.
Barratt, Harold. "Sam Selvon's Tiger: In Search of Self-Awareness." *Reworlding: The Literature of the Indian Diaspora*. Ed. E. S. Nelson. New York: Greenwood, 1992.
Barthes, Roland. *Critical Essays*. Trans. Richard Howard. Evanston, Ill.: Northwestern University Press, 1972.
_____. *Image, Music, Text*. Trans. Stephen Heath. New York: Hill and Wang, 1977.
Bhabha, Homi K. *The Location of Culture*. New York: Routledge, 1994.
Bissoondath, Neil. *A Casual Brutality*. New York: Penguin, 1989.
_____. *Digging Up the Mountains*. New York: Penguin, 1986.
_____. *Selling Illusions: The Cult of Multiculturalism in Canada*. Toronto: Penguin, 2002.
_____. *The Worlds Within Her*. London: William Heinemann, 1999.
Burton, Antoinette. *Cambridge History of Literary Criticism. Vol. 8 From Formalism to Poststructuralism*. Cambridge: Cambridge University Press, 1995.
_____. *Dwelling in the Archive*. New York: Oxford University Press, 2003.
Carb, Alison B. "An Interview with Bharati Mukherjee." *The Massachusetts Review*, 29.4 (1988): 645–654.
Caute, David. "Mehta." *Contemporary Literary Criticism*, Vol. 37. Detroit: Gale, 1986.
Chandra, Vikram. *Love and Longing in Bombay*. New York: Little, Brown, 1997.
_____. *Red Earth and Pouring Rain*. New York: Little, Brown, 1995.
Chhaya, Mayank. "Short, Succinct and Savory." http://www.literateworld.com/english/2002/bookshelf/july/bjul21.html, July 21 2002.
Chua, C.L. "Passages from India: Migrating to America in the Fiction of V.S. Naipaul and Bharati Mukherjee." *Reworlding: The Literature of the Indian Diaspora*. Ed. Emmanuel S. Nelson. Westport, Conn.: Greenwood, 1992.

Clarke, Colin, Ceri Peach, and Steven Vertovec, eds. *South Asians Overseas: Migration and Ethnicity.* Cambridge and New York: Cambridge University Press, 1990.
Crane, Ralph J. *Ruth Prawer Jhabvala.* New York: Twayne, 1992.
Derrida, Jacques. *Of Grammatology.* Trans. Gayatri Chakravorty Spivak. Baltimore: The Johns Hopkins University Press, 1976.
Desai, Anita. *Clear Light of Day.* London: Heinemann, 1980.
_____. *Fasting, Feasting.* New York: Houghton Mifflin, 1999.
Desai, Mahadev. "Books: Stories of Second Chances." *Khabar Magazine,* July 2001: 38.
Divakaruni, Chitra Banerjee. *Arranged Marriage.* New York: Anchor Books, 1995.
_____. *The Mistress of Spices.* New York: Anchor Books, 1997.
_____. *Sister of My Heart.* New York: Anchor Books, 1999.
_____. *The Unknown Errors of Our Lives.* New York: Doubleday, 2001.
_____. *The Vine of Desire.* New York: Doubleday, 2002.
Dowell, William, et al. "The Golden Diaspora." *Time,* June 19, 2000: B28.
Fanon, Frantz. *The Wretched of the Earth.* New York: Grove, 1963.
Feder, Lillian. *Naipaul's Truth: The Making of a Writer.* New York: Rowman and Littlefield, 2001.
Freire, Paulo. *The Pedagogy of the Oppressed.* New York: Continuum, 1993 (first published 1970).
Frye, Northrop. *Anatomy of Criticism: Four Essays.* Princeton: Princeton University Press, 1959.
Ghosh, Amitav. *The Calcutta Chromosome.* New York: Avon, 1995.
_____. *The Glass Palace.* New York: Random House, 2001.
Gordon, Leonard A. "Mehta." *Contemporary Literary Criticism.* Vol. 37. Detroit: Gale, 1986.
Grewal, Gurleen. "Born Again American: The Immigrant Consciousness in Jasmine." *Bharati Mukhenjee: Critical Perspectives,* E.S. Wilson, ed. New York: Garland, 1993.
Hardgrave, Robert L. Jr. "Mehta." *Contemporary Literary Criticism.* Vol. 37. Detroit: Gale, 1986.
Hayward, Helen. *The Enigma of V.S. Naipaul: Sources and Contexts.* New York: Palgrave Macmillan, 2002.
Hogan, Ron. "Akhil Sharma." *Beatrice Interviews.* www.beatrice.com./interviews/sharma/2000*: 1.
Hubel, Teresa. *Whose India?: The Independence Struggle in British and Indian Fiction and History.* Durham: Duke University Press, 1996.
Jablons, Pam. "Mehta." *Contemporary Literary Criticism.* Vol. 37. Detroit: Gale, 1986.
Jhabvala, Ruth Prawer. *Heat and Dust.* New York: Harper & Row, 1975.
_____. "How I Became a Holy Mother." *Out of India: Selected Stories.* New York: William Morrow, 1986.
_____. "The Interview." *Out of India: Selected Stories.* New York: William Morrow, 1986.
_____. "Passion." *Out of India: Selected Stories.* New York: William Morrow, 1986.

_____. "Two More Under the Indian Sun." *Out of India: Selected Stories*. New York: William Morrow, 1986.
Johnson, Gerald W. "Mehta." *Contemporary Literary Criticism*. Vol. 37. Detroit: Gale, 1986.
Jones, Mervyn. "Mehta." *Contemporary Literary Criticism*. Vol. 37. Detroit: Gale, 1986.
Joshi, Priya. *In Another Country: Colonialism, Culture, and the English Novel in India*. New York: Columbia University Press, 2002.
Julik, Rebecca. "Anita Desai." *Voices from the Gaps: Women Writers of Color*. Feb. 28, 1999 *http://voices.cla.umn.edu/authors/AnitaDesai.html*, Dec. 24, 2002.
Kanaganayakam, Chelva. *Counterrealism and Indo-Anglian Fiction*. Waterloo, Ont.: Wilfrid Laurier University Press, 2002.
Kapur, Manju. *Difficult Daughters*. London: Faber and Faber, 1998.
Kenny, Anthony. "Mehta." *Contemporary Literary Criticism*. Vol. 37. Detroit: Gale, 1986.
Kreisler, Harry. "Conversation with Author and Diplomat Shashi Tharoor," *Conversations with History*. Institute of International Studies, University of California, Berkeley: 1–5. *http://globetrotter.berkeley.edu/people/Tharoor/Tharoor—con3.html*, Jan 3, 2001.
Kumar, Amitava. *Bombay, London, New York*. New York: Routledge, 2002.
Ladoo, Harold Sonny. *No Pain Like This Body*. Toronto: Anansi, 1972.
_____. *Yesterdays*. Toronto: Anansi, 1974.
Lahiri, Jhumpa. "Contributors' Notes." *The Best American Short Stories 2000*. Ed. Katrina Kenison. New York: Houghton Mifflin, 2000.
_____. *Interpreter of Maladies: Stories*. New York: Houghton Mifflin, 1999.
Lessinger, Johanna. *From the Ganges to the Hudson: Indian Immigrants in New York City*. Boston: Allyn and Bacon, 1995.
Lichtenstein, David P. "A Brief Biography of V.S. Naipaul." Contributing editor, Caribbean Web. *www.postcolonial.org/stg.brown.edu/post/caribbean/naipaul/bio.html* July 26, 2000.
Lim, Shirley Geok-lin, ed. *Asian-American Literature*. Lincolnwood, Ill.: NTC, 2000.
Maharaj, Rabindranath. *Death of a Guru* (formerly *Escape into the Light*) with Dave Hunt. Eugene, Ore.: Harvest House, 1984.
_____. *The Writer and His Wife and Other Stories*. Leeds, Yorkshire: Peepal Tree, 1996.
Matthews, Herbert L. "Mehta." *Contemporary Literary Criticism*. Vol. 37. Detroit: Gale, 1986.
Mehta, Ved. *Continents of Exile: All for Love*. New York: Thunder's Mouth/ Nation Books, 2001.
_____. *Face to Face*. Boston: Little, Brown, 1957.
_____. *The Ledge Between the Streams*. New York: W.W. Norton, 1984.
_____. *Mamaji*. New York: Oxford University Press, 1979.
_____. *Sound-Shadows of the New World*. New York: W.W. Norton, 1985.
_____. *The Stolen Light*. New York: W.W. Norton, 1989.

_____. *A Ved Mehta Reader: The Craft of the Essay.* New Haven: Yale University Press, 1998.
_____. *Vedi.* New York: Oxford Univ. Press, 1982.
Mickley, Lisa. "Anita Rau Badami." Spring 1998. *http://www.emory.edu/ENGLISH/Bahri/Badami.html*, retrieved June 27, 2002.
Mistry, Rohinton. *Family Matters.* New York: Alfred A. Knopf, 2002.
_____. *A Fine Balance.* New York: Vintage, 1996.
_____. *Such a Long Journey.* New York: Vintage, 1992.
_____. *Swimming Lessons and other Stories from Firozsha Baag.* New York: Vintage, 1997.
Mitchell, Tom. "Rohinton Mistry." Fall 2000. *http://www.emory.edu/ENGLISH/Bahri/Mistry.html*, retrieved December 24, 2002.
Mukherjee, Bharati. *Darkness.* Markham, Ont.: Penguin, 1985.
_____. *Desirable Daughters.* New York: Hyperion, 2002.
_____. *The Holder of the World.* New York: Knopf, 1993.
_____. *Jasmine.* New York: Grove, 1989.
_____. *Leave It to Me.* New York: Ballantine, 1997.
_____. *The Middleman and Other Stories.* New York: Grove, 1988.
Mukerji, Dhan Gopal. *Caste and Outcast.* Stanford: Stanford University Press, 2002.
_____. *Gay-Neck: The Story of a Pigeon.* New York: Dutton Children's Books, 1927.
Naipaul, V.S. *The Enigma of Arrival.* New York: Alfred Knopf, 1987.
_____. *A House for Mr. Biswas.* London: Andre Deutsch, 1961.
_____. *In a Free State.* London: Andre Deutsch, 1971.
_____. *The Suffrage of Elvira.* London: Andre Deutsch, 1958.
_____. "Two Worlds." Nobel lecture. Dec. 7, 2001. *www.nobel.se/literaturelaureates/2001/naipaul.lecture*: 1–10.
Nelson, Emmanuel S. "Introduction." *Bharati Mukherjee: Critical Perspectives.* Ed. Emmanuel S. Nelson. New York: Garland, 1993.
Norgaard, Aja. "Up and Coming" (interview). Fall 1989. *http://aurora.icaap.org/archive/bissondath.html*, retrieved June 8, 2003.
Nossiter, Bernard. "Mehta." *Contemporary Literary Criticism.* Vol. 37. Detroit: Gale, 1986.
Parameswaran, Uma. "Dispelling the Spells of Memory: Another Approach to Reading our Yesterdays." *2000 Proceedings of the Red River Conference on World Literature.* Vol 2: 2000, retrieved November 7, 2003, pp. 1–20.
Pati (Wong), Mitali. "Love and the Indian Immigrant in Bharati Mukherjee's Short Fiction." *Bharati Mukherjee: Critical Perspectives.* Ed. Emmanuel S. Nelson. New York: Garland, 1993.
Perkins, Mitali. "An Interview with Myself." *http://www.mitaliperkins.com/aboutme.htm*, August 10, 2003.
_____. *The Sunita Experiment.* Boston: Little, Brown, 1993.
_____. "What's on Indian-American Author Mitali Perkins' Fire Escape." *http://www.mitaliperkins.com/fircontents.htm*, August 9, 2003.
Powers, Janet M. "Sociopolitical Critique as Indices and Narrative Codes in Bharati

Mukherjee's *Wife* and *Jasmine*." *Bharati Mukherjee: Critical Perspectives*. Ed. Emmanuel S. Nelson. New York: Garland, 1993.

Raghavan, Amit. "Vikram Seth." Spring 1999. *http://www.emory.edu/ENGLISH/Bahri/Seth.html*, Dec. 24, 2002.

Ramchand, Kenneth. *The West Indian Novel and Its Background*. New York: Barnes & Noble, 1970.

Ramraj, Victor. "Still Arriving: The Assimilationist Indo-Caribbean Experience of Marginality." *Reworlding: The Literature of the Indian Diaspora*. Ed. E. S. Nelson. New York: Greenwood, 1992.

Rana, Indi. *The Roller Birds of Rampur*. New York: Henry Holt, 1993.

Reeder, Allan. "A Conversation with Akhil Sharma." *The Atlantic Monthly*, January 1997. *www.theatlantic.com/unbound/factfict/asharma.htm*, retrieved January 2, 2001.

Salick, Roydon. *The Novels of Samuel Selvon: A Critical Study*. Westport, Conn.: Greenwood, 2001.

Scott, Paul. "Mehta." *Contemporary Literary Criticism*. Vol. 37. Detroit: Gale, 1986.

Selvon, Samuel. *A Brighter Sun*. London: A. Wingate, 1952.

_____. *The Plains of Caroni*. London: MacGibbon & Kee, 1970; Toronto: Williams-Wallace, 1986.

_____. *Turn Again Tiger*. London: MacGibbon & Kee, 1958.

Seth, Vikram. *A Suitable Boy*. New York: HarperCollins, 1993.

Sharma, Akhil. "Cosmopolitan." *The Best American Short Stories 1998*. Ed. Garrison Keillor with Katrina Kenison. New York: Houghton Mifflin, 1998.

_____. *An Obedient Father*. New York: Farrar, Strauss & Giroux, 2000.

Sharma, Maya Manju. "The Inner World of Bharati Mukherjee: From Expatriate to Immigrant." *Bharati Murkherjee: Critical Perspectives*, E.S. Wilson, ed. New York: Garland, 1993.

Sidhwa, Bapsi. *An American Brat*. Minneapolis, Minn.: Milkweed, 1993.

_____. *The Bride*. New York: St. Martin's, 1983.

_____. *Ice-Candy-Man*. (*Cracking India*) Minneapolis, Minn.: Milkweed, 1993.

Singer, Isaac Bashevis. Nobel lecture. Dec. 8, 1978. *www.nobel.se/literaturelaureates/1978/lsinger.lecture*: 1–3.

Singh, Rashna. *The Imperishable Empire: A Study of British Fiction in India*. Washington, D.C.: Three Continents, 1988.

"A Song of Lost Islands." *The Economist*, Dec. 10, 1994: 93.

Sonnenberg, Ben. "Tambimuttu in New York." *Bookend* in *The New York Times*, Sept. 21, 1997: 1–4. *www.nytimes.com/books/97/09/21/bookend/bookend.html*, retrieved January 5, 2002.

South Asian Journalists Association. "Vikram Chandra." Jan. 28, 1998, *http://www.saja.org/chandra.html*, Dec. 24, 2002.

Stone, Carole. "The Short Fictions of Bernard Malamud and Bharati Mukherjee." *Bharati Mukherjee: Critical Perspectives*. Ed. Emmanuel S. Nelson. New York: Garland, 1993.

Sucher, Laurie. *The Fiction of Ruth Prawer Jhabvala: The Politics of Passion*. New York: St. Martin's, 1989.

Sunday Guardian. Feb. 25, 2001. *www.nalis.gov.tt/Biography/NeilBissoondath.htm*, retrieved June 8, 2003.

Suri, Manil. *The Death of Vishnu*. New York: HarperCollins, 2001.

Tambimutttu, Thurairajah, and Richard March, eds. *T.S. Eliot: A Symposium*. London: Editions Poetry London, 1948.

Trivedi, Nirmal. Review of *The Hero's Walk*. *http://www.popmatters.com/books/reviews/heros-walk.html*, July 3, 2003.

"UK writer Naipaul wins Nobel award." October 11, 2001. cnn.com/SPECIALS/2001/nobel: 1–2, retrieved January 4, 2002.

Upadhyay, Samrat. "Arranged Marriage: Between Third World and First." *Review of Books*, Oct. 26, 1997. *The Kathmandu Post. www.south-asia.com/Ktmpost/1997/Oct/Oct26-ed.html*: 2–4.

———. "The Good Shopkeeper." *The Best American Short Stories 1999*. Ed. Amy Tan with Katrina Kenison. New York: Houghton Mifflin, 1999.

Wain, John. "Mehta." *Contemporary Literary Criticism*. Vol. 37. Detroit: Gale, 1986.

Wallia, C.J.S. "Dhan Gopal Mukerji's *Caste and Outcast*." *IndiaStar Review of Books*, *http://www.indiastar.com/wallia31.htm*, August 9, 2003.

Wong, Eugene F. *On Visual Media Racism: Asians in the American Motion Pictures*. New York: Arno, 1978.

Woolf, Virginia. "A Room of One's Own." *The Norton Anthology of English Literature*. 7th edition. New York: Norton, 2001.

Zaman, Niaz. *A Divided Legacy: The Partition in Selected Novels of India, Pakistan, and Bangladesh*. Dhaka: The University Press Ltd., 1999.

Index

The Adventures of Augie March (Bellow) 14
Alexander, Meena 9
An American Brat (Sidhwa) 78–79
Anglo-Indian 119
anti–Asian racism 14
anxiety of existence 119, 121
Arranged Marriage (Divakaruni) 64–66
As I Lay Dying (Faulkner) 88
Asians' desire to return 23

Badami, Anita Rau 13, 110–112
Bellow, Saul 14
Bissoondath, Neil 103, 104, 106, 109
The Book of Ifs and Buts (Maharaj) 109
The Bride (Sidhwa) 74, 77, 78
A Brighter Sun (Selvon) 24, 25, 26

The Calcutta Chromosome (Ghosh) 63, 94–95
Caste and Outcast (Mukerji, D.G.) 8
A Casual Brutality (Bissoondath) 106, 108
Chandra, Vikram 13, 89, 100–102
Charlotte's Web (E.B. White) 120
The Circle of Reason (Ghosh) 94
Clear Light of Day (Desai) 91
Continents of Exile (Mehta) 40–42
"Cosmopolitan" (Sharma) 83–84
Cracking India (Sidhwa) 74–76
The Crow Eaters (Sidhwa) 77

Daddyji (Mehta) 30
The Dangling Man (Bellow) 14
Darkness (Mukherjee) 50, 54, 55, 56
A Daughter of the Narikin (Sugimoto) 9

A Daughter of the Nohfu (Sugimoto) 9
Days and Nights in Calcutta (Mukherjee, B.) 50, 53
Dear Mr. Henshaw (Cleary) 121
Death of a Guru or Escape Into the Light (Maharaj) 109, 110
The Death of Vishnu (Suri) 113
Delinquent Chacha (Mehta) 30, 38
Desai, Anita 13, 89, 90–93, 98; prolific fiction 90
Desirable Daughters (Mukherjee, B.) 50, 62–63
Difficult Daughters (Kapur) 98–100
Digging Up the Mountains (Bissoondath) 106, 107, 108
Divakaruni, Chitra 9, 13, 14, 49

educated reading public 9, 10
The Enigma of Arrival (Naipaul) 17, 18
Eliot, T.S. 5, 8

Face to Face (Mehta) 30, 32–34, 35
A Family Affair (Mehta) 30, 32
Family Matters (Mistry) 112, 115–117
Fasting, Feasting (Desai) 91–93
Faulkner, William 88
A Fine Balance (Mistry) 112, 114–115
Fly and the Fly Bottle (Mehta) 30–31

Gay-Neck, the Story of a Pigeon (Mukerji, D.G.) 8, 119–121
gender roles 14
The Glass Palace (Ghosh) 95, 97
Ghosh, Amitav 13, 89, 93–97
"The Good Shopkeeper" (Upadhyay) 83

Index

The Great Indian Novel (Tharoor) 13

Hari the Jungle Lord (Mukherji, D.G.) 119
Heat and Dust (Jhabvala) 46–48
The Hero's Walk (Badami) 111, 112
Herzog (Bellow) 14
The Holder of the World (Mukherjee, B.) 50, 52, 59–61
Homer in Flight (Maharaj) 109
A House for Mr. Biswas (Naipaul) 20–22
"How I Became a Holy Mother" (Jhabvala) 46
The Hunchback of Notre Dame (Hugo) 114

"In a Free State" (Naipaul) 18
In Antique Land (Ghosh) 94
Indo-Anglian 6, 15, 16
Indo-Caribbean 16, 103, 104
The Interloper (Maharaj) 109
The Interpreter of Maladies (Lahiri) 69, 80–82
"The Interview" (Jhabvala) 43
Iyer, Pico 9

Jasmine (Mukherjee, B.) 50, 52, 57–58
Jhabvala, Ruth Prawer 29, 42–48
Joy Luck Club (Tan) 14
The Jungle Book (Kipling) 119

Kapur, Manju 13, 89, 98–100
Kari the Elephant (Mukerji, D.G.) 119
Kingston, Maxine Hong 14
The Kitchen God's Wife (Tan) 14

Ladoo, Harold Sonny 103, 104–106
The Lagahoo's Apprentice (Maharaj) 109
Lahiri, Jhumpa 15, 79–82
Leave It to Me (Mukherjee, B.) 50, 61–62
The Ledge Between the Streams (Mehta) 30, 38, 39–40
Love and Longing in Bombay (Chandra) 101–102, 113

Maharaj, Rabindranath 109
Mahatma and His Apostles (Mehta) 30, 32
Mamaji (Mehta) 30, 35

Mehta, Ved 5, 7, 13, 29–42, 30
The Middleman and Other Stories (Mukherjee) 50, 54, 56, 57
The Mistress of Spices (Divakaruni) 66–68
Mistry, Rohinton 13, 103, 112–117
Mukerji, Dhan Gopal 8, 9, 119–121
Mukherjee, Bharati 6, 13, 14, 49, 63

Naipaul, V. S. 5, 6, 7, 13, 14, 16, 16–22, 106
The New India (Mehta) 30, 32
New Theologian (Mehta) 30, 31
The New Yorker 5, 7, 13, 29, 30, 41, 80, 83
Newbery Medal 8, 119
No Pain Like This Body (Ladoo) 104–105

An Obedient Father (Sharma) 84–86
The Old Man and the Sea (Hemingway) 24
"One But of Many" (Naipaul) 18–19
otherness or marginalit 14, 15
Out of India (Jhabvala) 44

"Passion" (Jhabvala) 44–45
Perkins, Mitali 13, 119, 121, 124–127
The Plains of Caroni (Selvon) 24
the plurality of narratives 12
Poetry London 8
Poetry London—New York 8
Portrait of India (Mehta) 30, 31
post-colonialist criticism 7
post-colonialists 6, 7, 15, 44
Potter, Beatrix 120
psychological verisimilitude 118

questions of canon 118

Rana, Indi 13, 119, 121–124
Red Earth and Pouring Rain (Chandra) 100–101
The Roller Birds of Rampur (Rana) 5, 121–124, 126
Rowling, J.K. 121

SACLIT 103
Selling Illusions (Bissoondath) 106–107
Selvon, Samuel 7, 14, 16, 22–28
Seth, Vikram 89, 97–98
The Shadow Lines (Ghosh) 94

Sharma, Akhil 5, 13, 15, 73, 83–86
shlemiels (losers) 15, 42, 52
Sidhwa, Bapsi 73–79
Singer, Isaac Bashevis 14
Sister of My Heart (Divakaruni) 68–69, 71
The Sorrow and the Terror (Mukherjee, B.) 50
Sound Shadows of the New World 30, 36, 38
South Asian male as a sex object 43, 44, 45, 46
South Asian migration 9, 10, 11
The Stolen Light (Mehta) 37, 38
subordination of women 14
Such a Long Journey (Mistry) 112, 114
The Suffrage of Elvira (Naipaul) 19, 20
Sugimoto, Etsu 9
A Suitable Boy (Seth) 89, 97–98
The Sunita Experiment (Perkins) 5, 124–127
Suri, Manil 73, 86–88, 113, 114
Swimming Lessons and Other Stories from Firozsha Baag (Mistry) 112, 113–114

Tamarind Mem (Badami) 110, 111
Tambimuttu, Thurairajah 8
Tan, Amy 14

Tharoor, Shashi 13
The Tiger's Daughter (Mukherjee, B.) 50, 51, 52 53
Turn Again Tiger (Selvon) 24, 26, 27, 28
"Two More Under the Indian Sun" (Jhabvala) 45–46

The Unknown Errors of Our Lives (Divakaruni) 69–70
Upadhyay, Samrat 5, 15, 73, 82

Vedi (Mehta) 30, 35, 36
The Velveteen Rabbit (Williams, Margery) 120
The Victim (Bellow) 14
The Vine of Desire (Divakaruni) 70–71

Walking the Indian Streets (Mehta) 30, 34
Wife (Mukherjee, B.) 50, 51, 52, 53–54
Winnie the Pooh (Milne) 120
The Woman Warrior (Kingston) 14
Worlds Within Her (Bissoondath) 106, 108, 109
The Writer and His Wife (Maharaj) 109

Yesterdays (Ladoo) 105–106

www.ingramcontent.com/pod-product-compliance
Lightning Source LLC
Chambersburg PA
CBHW032105300426
44116CB00007B/894